Table of Contents

GW00480601

PRELUDE

Table of contents

Unhappy humans

LOVE YOURSELF UNCONDITIONALLY

    Self-Love is unconditional love.

CONFIDENCE

    Confidence rule ONE

    Confidence Rule TWO

    Confidence rule THREE

    Confidence rule FOUR

        Confidence rule FIVE

    Confidence rule SIX

    Confidence rule SEVEN

    Confidence rule EIGHT

    Confidence Rule NINE

    Confidence Rule TEN

    Confidence Rule ELEVEN

    GET TO KNOW YOURSELF

    THE GOOD STUFF

    You've been there since day one

    Your worth isn't determined by your looks

    Don't punish yourself

    YOU'RE THE BOSS OF YOUR LIFE

        DON'T PILE YOUR PROBLEMS INTO ONE PILE

Determining your self-worth

Society

Controlled by Society

I Hate Myself

LIFE SUCK SOMETIMES

Today is a new day for you. It's the beginning of a new chapter in your life

5 REASONS PEOPLE DON'T LOVE THEMSELVES

LOVE AS YOU KNOW IT

THE FIRST STEP IN LOVING YOURSELF

THE SECOND STEP

THE THIRD STEP

THE FOURTH STEP

THE FIFTH STEP

Treat yourself right

Raining on your own parade

THE SIXTH STEP

THE SEVENTH STEP

THE EIGHTH STEP

A haters job is to HATE you

THE NINTH STEP

Who you really are

THE TENTH STEP

THE ELEVENTH STEP

THE TWELFTH STEP

THE THIRTEENTH STEP

THE FOURTEENTH STEP

THE FIFTEENTH STEP

THE SIXTEENTH STEP

THE SEVENTEENTH STEP

THE EIGHTEENTH STEP

THE NINETEENTH STEP

THE TWENTIETH STEP

The TWENTY FIRST STEP

THE TWENTY SECOND STEP

THE TWENTY THIRD STEP

THE TWENTY FOURTH STEP

THE TWENTY FIFTH STEP

THE TWENTY SIXTH STEP

THE TWENTY SEVENTH STEP

THE TWENTY EIGHTH STEP

The TWENTY NINTH STEP

Happiness

THE THIRTIETH STEP

THE THIRTY FIRST STEP

THE THIRTY SECOND STEP

THE THIRTY THIRD STEP

THE THIRTY FOURTH STEP

THE THIRTY FIFTH STEP

PRELUDE

If you don't learn how to love yourself, you'll be miserable forever. You'll also float through life like a robot that's programmed to live instead of like a person that is choosing to live. There's a big difference between living your life, and wasting it away. When you're living your life you can't wait to wake up in the morning and go after your dreams. When you're wasting your life away you get up because you have to, and you just go through life like a zombie. When you're wasting your life away you don't care about yourself, and you give up on a lot of things in life. Also, you do things because you have to not because you want to. So, are you living your life or wasting it away? If you're pretending to be happy even though you're miserable inside chances are you're not living your life to the fullest. A fake smile can fool the world, but it can't fool the person behind the smile. Stop pretending to be happy, and find a way to be happy. You can pretend that everything is okay, but until you deal with what's bothering you it won't go away. Life is better when you're happy to be alive, and you're living your life to the fullest. Life is better when you're going after your dreams, and you're chasing after happiness. Life is better when you're happy, and you love yourself and your life. This guide gives you 35 things you must do in order to love yourself and your life. If you don't learn how to love yourself, you'll never find happiness because finding happiness starts with being happy with yourself

Unhappy humans

What you have to realize is that no-one is perfect everyone on this earth has flaws, and everyone on this earth has something that they hate about themselves. If someone were perfect they would still think that something was wrong with them. To be honest, humans are never happy with what they've got. It's always going to be something you're going to want to change, and there's always going to be something you're going to want to do differently. Its like, have you ever wanted something really bad, and you finally got it, and you were happy with it for a while until something newer came out, and then you wanted that instead? It's just like that, people are always wanting something they can't have or don't have, and when they get it they want something else. People with super huge breast want smaller breast, and people with smaller breast want bigger breast. People that are tall want to be shorter and people that are short want to be taller. It's always the opposite. People are never 100% happy with who they are. I mean why can't you just be happy with who you are? Oh yeah, it's because you constantly dream about being a perfect person with a perfect everything. However, you need to realize that perfect people don't exist. Therefore, you'll never be perfect, but that's perfectly fine because being imperfect is normal. However, even though you'll never be perfect you can still be happy.

LOVE YOURSELF UNCONDITIONALLY

Some people put conditions on their love.

They say that they can't or won't love themselves:

1. Until they lose weight or gain weight

2. Until they get rid of a flaw that they have

3. Until they achieve their goals

4. Until they win someone else's approval

5. Until something about themselves or their life changes

Never tell yourself that you can't or won't love yourself until one of the above things happens. That's an unfair and cruel ultimatum to tell anyone.

Would you ever tell a loved one of the following things?

1. I won't love you until you gain weight or lose weight _____

2. I won't love you until you get rid of that flaw _____

3. I won't love you until you reach your goals or dreams _____

4. I won't love you until you change the way that you look? _____

5. Do you tell yourself that you won't love yourself until you change or do something?

_____

6. What do you tell yourself that you have to change, in order for you to love yourself?

_____

_____

_____

Chances are you wouldn't tell anyone you love the above things because you know it's cruel, and unfair. Also, you love them no matter what. Basically, you love them unconditionally. Starting right now give yourself unconditional love, love without ultimatums and cruel demands.

Self-Love is unconditional love.

Realize that no-one can love you better than you can love yourself. You're the one person that knows every flaw, weakness, and secret that you have. You're the only person that can't ever leave you. You're the only person that knows your every desire, thought and emotion. Therefore, when you love yourself it really is unconditional love.

- Be the one person in your life that doesn't judge you.

- Be the one person in your life that loves you for you.

- Be the one person in your life that has your back no matter what.

- Be the one person in your life that doesn't judge you because of your looks.

- Be the one person in your life that you can count on no matter what.

- Be your own cheerleader, your own best friend, and your own supporter.

From now on will you show yourself conditional love or unconditional love?

_____

CONFIDENCE

Confidence is an important part of loving yourself. Therefore, before I delve deeper into how you can love yourself I want to give you a few pointers on building your confidence as well.

Do you consider yourself to be a confident person? _____

Confidence is an important attribute to have. Confident people stand out and they aren't afraid to be themselves. It's easy to spot people that have low self-esteem because they usually walk around with their head down, they barely make eye contact, and they're constantly looking around to see if anyone is judging them. A confident person walks with their head held high, they aren't afraid to make eye contact, and they don't care if people around them are judging them. For starters, I 'd like to say that I used to be the shy girl that was afraid of being judged as well, but now I'm more confident and I'm far from shy. How did I go from being a shy girl that was afraid to speak in small group settings; to a girl that doesn't have a problem speaking to a crowd of people? Well, I just started being true to myself. I stopped caring about what society expected of me and I started caring about what I wanted. My expectations became a priority, and societies expectations became an option. Don't be afraid to go against society. You were born an individual and you don't have to conform to everything. You have your own brain and mouth for a reason. So, use them. If everyone was supposed to think the same things we'd all share the same brain. Once you stop caring about what society will think of you, you become an individual that isn't afraid to be themselves. A confident individual that isn't afraid to speak up and stand up for themselves.

First of all, confidence starts from the inside, not the outside. A person can change their whole appearance and still not have confidence. Until a person fixes issues that they have emotionally, and mentally their confidence will remain low. The most beautiful woman in the world could have low self-esteem because self-esteem is based on what she thinks of herself and not what everyone in the world thinks of her.

People aren't born with low self-esteem. Something happens to them while they're growing up that causes their self-esteem to drop. In order for you to build your confidence, you have to start from the beginning. Where did your low self-esteem come from?

Here is a list of common reasons that cause people to develop low self-esteem:

1. Their peers made fun of them

2. They hate their appearance?

3. They constantly get rejected?

4. They've never been loved?

5. They've been hurt or abused?

6. They hate their flaws?

7. Their parents didn't love them or show them love?

8. Their parents didn't or doesn't accept them?

9. Someone they loved left them or rejected them?

10. They feel alone and as if no-one cares about them?

11. People are always looking at them strangely in public.

12. They feel as if they don't fit in or belong.

13. They don't feel accepted by their peers.

14. They were in a relationship with someone that mistreated them.

15. They were in a relationship with someone that treated them liked they weren't good enough.

16. They are currently in love with someone that acts like they aren't good enough

17. They don't think they're good enough.

18. They constantly compare themselves to others that they think are more successful or attractive than they are

- What number(s) apply to you? _____

- The numbers that apply to you are areas that you need to work on.

- If you don't work on those things your self-esteem won't approve.

Confidence rule ONE

Stay True to yourself

No matter what happens to you in life don't let anyone or anything change who you really are. If you're a nice person don't let anyone change you into a mean, hateful person. Never turn into the monster that hurt you. After someone hurts you it's hard not to change your personality, but it's not impossible. Always remember that you're strong enough to move forward without changing into someone that you're not. Who are you inside? Are you staying true to who you are inside? Have you changed into someone you're not because of what happened to you in the past? Most people change because they want to protect themselves from being hurt again. They act mean and put up a wall because they want to keep the bad people out. They don't trust anyone, and they keep people at a distance. Breathe in and breathe out. Breathe in and breathe out. I know what happened to you in the past hurts you, and it's quite painful, but you can't let it change you into someone that you're not. You're better than that. Realize that everyone in the world isn't bad, and everyone in the world isn't out to get you. There are nice people out there that are hurting just like you are, and they're looking for someone to love not hurt. Everyone isn't the same, you've just ran into too many negative people in your lifetime. Try not to be negative towards other people. Try not to be the monster that hurts someone else.

1. Do you want to be like the person that hurt you? _____

2. Do you want to be the positive person in someone's life or the negative person in someone's

   life? _____

3. Do you want to build people up or tear them down? _____

Also, live your life for you, not for anyone else. Don't let the fear of being judged, rejected or disliked stop you from being yourself. Don't pretend to be someone else just to get people to like you. Don't hide who you really are just to win someone else's approval. If they don't approve of you or your choices that's their problem, not yours.

Did your parents give you unconditional love? _____

In a perfect world, every parent would love their child no matter what. However, some parents won't love you or care about your wellbeing. Realize that it's not your fault that your parents aren't loving you like a parent should. Sure it hurts, but you have to realize that some parents aren't fit to be parents, and if you ever have children make sure that you don't treat them like your parents treated you. Also, some parents won't approve of your life choices. So, you just have to live your life without their approval. Unless you've done something extremely horrible, I mean you've committed heinous crimes or mistreated your parents in the worst way there's no excuse for them to not show you love. However, don't expect your parents to approve of everything you do. Your parents might have their ow beliefs, and their beliefs might not align with yours. So, you both have to agree to disagree and let e other live their own life. Although your parents won't approve of everything you do or say they should still love you anyway. Just like you might not agree with their views, but you still love them and want them in your life.

Realize that you won't always have everyone's approval and that you won't always be loved back, but you should still stay true to yourself. Life's too short to be unhappy. Do you and be you, and if people don't like you or the way that you live your life that's their problem, not yours. Your life will still go on and on and on. It's better to be yourself and live a happy life than it is to pretend to be someone else and live a miserable life. Which is more important to you; winning the approval of others or staying true to yourself and being happy? If someone leaves you because they don't like who you are they don't belong in your life. Realize that you weren't born to please everyone in your life. It's your life and what you do with your life should be your choice. The only life someone else should be controlling is their own life; don't let them control yours. Are you staying true to yourself or are you living your life the way that someone else wants you to live it? You only get one life, and you're the one that should be writing your life story. If someone else is writing it for you, it's time for you to take the pen out of their hand and start writing it yourself. The story will become more fun and exciting when you start writing what the main character does or doesn't do. "Realize that your real friends and family will love you no matter what."

Always remember that you decide who you want to be. NEVER let someone else decide who you will be and how you will act.

Confidence Rule TWO

Are you afraid to speak in front of a room full of people? _____

Realize that you have a voice

Your opinion does matter. Always take advantage of your freedom of speech. If you disagree with something let it be known. You have a mouth and a brain for a reason. When you're shy you're afraid to speak up because people will look at you, you don't like being the center of attention, and you're afraid of saying the wrong thing and being judged. From now on if the words want to come out let them come out. Let your words escape from your lips. When you speak people will stare at you, but it's only to hear what you have to say. If they don't like what you have to say that's their problem, not yours. Life is better when you're not afraid to speak up and be heard. People have died for you to be able to have freedom of speech. Some people still don't have the right to freedom of speech. If you have it, use it. What do you have to say? What do you want the world to know? Why are you living in silence? Shy people have a lot to say, but they're afraid to say it. Say it, and stop worrying about what others will think of it. If it's your opinion, then it is your opinion. So what if others disagree with it? The next time you have something to say don't hold it in, just open your mouth and say it. If you say it no-one is going to kill you, and the world isn't going to end. The worst that could happen is that someone will disagree with you, but hey not everyone will agree with everything you say. Just agree to disagree and move on.

1. When you're having a group discussion chime in and give your opinion. Your opinion is just as important as everyone else's opinion.

2. If you don't agree with something speak up because silence can be seen as agreeing. If you don't agree speak up or they will assume that you agree.

3. Take advantage of your freedom of speech.

4. Jump into conversations with these lead in words 'I think', 'In my opinion'. These lead in words are great for those who are nervous about giving their opinion or for those that are afraid to speak up because they want to avoid a confrontation.

5. Start off a speech with a joke or humor. It will lighten the mood in the room.

6. Realize that people aren't always listening to judge you and that it's okay to be a little nervous or mess up. When you mess up, correct yourself and keep on going or just laugh it off.

Some people are afraid to speak their mind because they're afraid of confrontation. They don't want people to get mad at them or they're afraid of what people will do to them. Realize that not standing up for yourself can lead to you being walked over. Some people don't respect those who don't stand up for themselves.

Jane told Tom to shut up. Tom shut up and sat down.

Jane told Jason to shut up. Jason said 'no', and told her not to speak to him that way.

1. Which guy will Jane continue to tell to shut up?

2. Which guy will Jane walk all over?

3. Which guy will Jane think is a pushover?

4. Which guy will Jane DISRESPECT?

5. Which guy will Jane respect?

Don't be afraid of confrontation. If you're afraid that someone will hit you then you shouldn't be dealing with that person in the first place. If you're afraid of not being liked you should realize that not standing up for yourself causes people to think you're weak, and a pushover. So, not speaking up for yourself isn't helping you to be liked. In fact, most people respect those who speak their mind and have an opinion. Confident people aren't afraid to say what's on their mind, and they don't care if others agree with them or not. In group conversations, confident people lead the conversation and tend to be in control of what the group will do. Confident people aren't afraid of confronting people that have wronged them. The only reason that you shouldn't confront someone is if you know they're a violent person. In that case, you need to separate yourself from them

Don't be afraid to stand up for yourself and defend yourself. Tell people to stop doing things that are hurtful. Tell people what you like or dislike. If you disagree with something let it be known. Set your thoughts free. Life is better when you don't hold everything in.

Will you speak your mind from now on? _____

Will you stand up for yourself from now on? _____

Confidence rule THREE

Be a leader, not a follower.

Confident people like to lead. Shy people want to lead but they don't have enough confidence. From now on if you have the opportunity to lead take it. If you have a lot of great ideas, and you know you'd be great at being the leader don't let your shyness stop you from taking the lead. If you're great at something and you refuse to show it off or use it to your advantage you're holding yourself back. Sometimes shy people are afraid to take the lead because they don't think others will like their ideas, and they're afraid of being rejected. However, some shy people are afraid to lead because they don't want to be blamed for a failed project. Well, whether you're the leader or the follower in the group you're still a part of the group and everyone in the group will be blamed for it failing. However, depending on the situation or setting the leader might receive most of the blame. Realize that failing is a part of growing. If you never fail, you'll never know what your weaknesses are and you'll never be able to improve yourself. When you fail, realize that it's not the end of the world. Examine why you failed and use your failure as a learning experience. When a person learns from their failures they grow and become a better person. Realize that everything won't be a success and that everything won't be a failure. Sometimes you'll succeed and sometimes you'll fail. Failing won't kill you. Failing isn't the end of the world. If you fail something, try it again or try something else. Confident people know they'll fail at some things and succeed at other things. However, they don't let their past failures stop them from chasing after success. To them, every day is another chance to start over, and every day is another chance to try something new. Yesterday's failure has nothing to do with what they'll do tomorrow or a week from now on.

Will you take the lead sometimes and not just follow? _____

Confidence rule FOUR

Confident people know that every day isn't going to be a good day. Some people with low self-esteem can't handle bad days. If their day isn't going well their self-esteem drops even lower. Stop expecting every day to be a good day. In reality, you will have bad days, bad weeks, bad months or even a bad year. Life can suck sometimes, but you should never let what happens to you stop you from chasing after what you want in life. There are thousands of success stories that prove that a person can go from poor to rich, from bad years to good years, and from being unknown to a celebrity. What happens today doesn't always determine what will happen tomorrow. The bad day will last for 24 hours and then you'll wake up the next day and be able to start over again. Sometimes it will seem like every day is a bad day, but if you keep fighting you'll have good days again. Learn from your bad days, and enjoy your good days. What happened on that bad day that you can learn from? What happened on that bad day that you can stop from happening again? Think about all of those bad days you had before. Did any of those bad days kill you? Think about all of those good days you had before? Those good days were fun and those good days prove that life isn't that bad. You'll have good days and you'll have bad days, and if you keep fighting you'll have better days.

What 3 moments in your life made you really happy?

1.

_____

_____

2.

_____

_____

3.

_____

_____

Confidence rule FIVE

Realize that if IT'S NOT GOING TO KILL YOU there's no need to be afraid of it and there's no need to avoid it.

1. People staring at you in public places WON'T KILL YOU

2. Speaking your mind and people not liking what you say WON'T KILL YOU.

3. People making fun of you WON'T KILL YOU

4. People not liking you WON'T KILL YOU.

5. Speaking in front of a group of people WON'T KILL YOU.

6. There's no point in being afraid of things that WON'T KILL YOU.

Sure some of these things will be embarrassing or hurtful but it won't kill you. REALIZE that you've survived worse things than the things I mentioned above.

1. If someone doesn't agree with you what's the worst that could happen?

_____

2. If someone stares at you what's the worst that can happen?

_____

3. If a stranger doesn't like you or what they see what's the worst that can happen?

_____

4. If you fall or fail in front of a group of people what's the worst that can happen?

_____

What you have to realize is that you are exaggerating what will and can happen to you when certain things happen. The most that can happen is something small but you're imagining it being or becoming something BIG or worse than it will be. From now on be realistic about what will and can happen, and if it won't KILL YOU don't let it STOP you from being you or doing it.

From now on will you let fear stop you from doing things that won't kill you? _____

Confidence rule SIX

Do you like when people stare at you?

_____

Why do you think people stare at you?

_____

_____

Is to stop transferring or projecting the negative feelings you have about yourself onto other people. A lot of people with low self-esteem walk around with a bunch of negative thoughts in their head and they assume that everyone that stares at them is thinking those things when in reality they're the one that's thinking those things. For example; if I'm having a bad hair day I'd think that everyone that stares at me is looking at my hair and thinking negative things about my hair. A person who hates a lot of things about themselves will assume that people are staring at them because of those things. If you hate your lips, you'll assume that people are staring at you because of your lips. If you hate your nose you'll assume that everyone is staring at you because of your nose. I think you get the point. However, you need to realize that everyone that looks at you isn't thinking those things. YOU'RE the one that's thinking those things and you're projecting it onto other people. You're basically writing a script for everyone that looks at you. As soon as they look at you, the negative voice in your head speaks what you imagine that they are thinking. What you have to realize is that most of the strangers you run into in public aren't thinking about you at all. They are busy living their life. The next time you go out in public look around at what everyone else is doing. What you'll realize is that most people are focused on themselves and what they're doing. If they do look at you, it will only be for a moment and then they'll return to what they're doing. The next time you go out in public don't write scripts for people just do what you came to do. Wave at a few people and say 'hi' and you'll realize that most people will return the gesture. Smile at a few people and you'll realize that most will wave or smile back. Once you start doing more positive things towards the strangers you meet in public you'll realize that most people aren't negative and that they'd actually respond to you in a positive manner. Also, you'd realize that the script you are writing for most people isn't true at all.

Also, realize that strangers are people you might not ever see again. Don't drive yourself crazy worrying about the opinion of someone you might not ever see again. As soon as they leave the store, gas station or wherever you run into them at they won't be thinking about you. People have their own life and they aren't going to be thinking about a stranger they walked past at the grocery store. No offense, but unless you're a celebrity being chased by paparazzi strangers aren't going to be thinking about you after they leave the mall or other public places they've run into you at. So, try not to over exaggerate the outcome of situations.

Have you been projecting your thoughts about yourself onto others? _____

Will you try to stop projecting your thoughts about yourself onto others? _____

Confidence rule SEVEN

Do you walk into a room full of a people with a positive attitude or a negative attitude?

_____

Bring the positivity not the negativity

Confident people walk into a room and they show everyone positivity. They walk into a room with a positive attitude, not a negative attitude. If I walk into a room and say 'Hey Everyone' with a smile on my face, people will think I'm friendly and approachable. If I walk into a room with my head down and a scowl on my face, and I don't speak to anyone people will assume that I'm unfriendly and unapproachable. People with low self-esteem tend to think negative thoughts when they enter into a room. Anxiety kicks in and they assume that something bad is going to happen to them or that people won't accept them. So, to avoid any negativity they put their guard up or avoid people or certain situations that they think will turn out negatively. However, what they need to realize is that they're the ones that are making the situation or environment negative. Walking into a room and not being friendly is creating a negative environment. I'm not saying that you have to walk into a room or building and be bubbly, but I am saying that you should be welcoming and open. If you're afraid to speak to everyone in the room, just walk in and wave. If you're walking into a store just look around and get busy doing what you came to do; don't walk into the store with a scowl on your face like you're ready to attack anyone that looks at you. Realize that you're the one causing most of the negativity that you're trying to avoid. Enter places with a positive attitude and chances are you'll have a positive experience. Enter places with a negative attitude and chances are you'll have a negative experience. If you're constantly thinking that everyone is out to get you and that every encounter that you have with others is going to turn into a negative situation that is going to harm you I suggest that you talk to a licensed psychologist.

Confidence rule EIGHT

Build a list of things that can't be taken away from you.

Most confident people have qualities that can't be taken away from them. No matter how many people hate them or bash them those qualities or accomplishments can't be stripped away from them. Thousands or millions of people hate Obama, but they can't take away the fact that he's the President. That's an accomplishment that they can't take away from him.

Realize that there are some things in life that people can't take away from you. An ex of mine called me 'stupid', and I had no choice but to laugh at him. First of all, he was constantly asking me how to spell things, and secondly, my GPA was and still is high. So, no matter how many times he or anyone else calls me stupid they can't erase my GPA and other things that prove that I'm not stupid. I love that there are a lot of good things about me that no-one can take away from me. What are some good things about you that no-one can take away from you? No matter what they say about you, they can't erase those things. If a celebrity sells a million records, and a thousand people state that they hate the record. They still can't change the fact that the celebrity sold a million records or that the celebrity is famous, rich, and successful. Your talents and your accomplishments can't be taken away from you no matter what anyone thinks or says about you.

1. What are your talents? Are you using your talents to the best of your ability?

_____

_____

_____

_____

2. What are your goals and dreams? Are you chasing after your goals and dreams?

_____

_____

_____

_____

3. What are some things about you that no-one can take away from you?

_____

_____

_____

_____

4. What can you do to add more things to your list of accomplishments?

_____

_____

_____

_____

Basically, work on achieving your goals and dreams because if you're unhappy with your life it will damage your self-esteem. If you're disappointed with your life make changes in your life asap. Once you do you'll be proud of yourself instead of disappointed. In my book '29 Steps to Getting Your Life Back On The Right Track' I tell you how to achieve your goals.

Confidence Rule NINE

Do you walk with your head up or down? _____

Do you avoid making eye contact with strangers? _____

      Confident people walk with their shoulders back and their head held high. This shows confidence and it shows that you're not hiding from anyone. So, roll your shoulders back and hold your head up high. People with low self-esteem tend to hold their head down when they're approaching people that they feel inferior to or people that they think will judge them. Realize that everyone on the planet is equal to you. You're not inferior to anyone. Don't bow your head down for anyone. I don't care who someone else is or what they've accomplished, their life isn't worth more than your life. Also, if they want to judge you holding your head down isn't going to stop them from doing it. I will discuss being judged in another step. So, when you're out in public don't hide from anyone by holding your head down.

      At first walking around with your head held high will seem awkward, but after a while, you'll get used to it. Tip for beginners; if you're walking into a store or public place glance around the room without targeting a specific person, and just focus on what you came for. Just make sure that you're holding your head up at all times. Also, making eye contact will become easier as your confidence rises.

      From now on will you walk with your head up? _____

Confidence Rule TEN

      Work with what you've got.

Confident people highlight their best qualities and work on making what they already have even better. Some people with low self-esteem tend to let their weaknesses and flaws dominate their life. However, confident people don't let their weaknesses or poor qualities control or dominate their life. Confident people let their strengths, accomplishments, and talents dominant their life. Basically, you have to work with what you've got and work on improving the things you can improve on.

1. What are you good at and how can you make it even better?

_____

_____

_____

2. What are your best qualities or characteristics and how can you highlight them?

_____

_____

_____

Work with what you've got.

1. What celebrity has some of the same flaws, qualities or imperfections that you have?

_____

2. Did they use that as an excuse to stop them from reaching their goals?

_____

3. Should you use your flaws or imperfections as an excuse for not reaching your goals?

_____

A lot of famous or successful people came from poor homes or they have health issues or they have some of the same problems or flaws that you might have, but they're not letting it stop them. Basically, they are working with what they've got, and guess what…. you have to do the same. In my book 'I Love Me and I Know My Worth' I go over this in more detail.

Confidence Rule ELEVEN

Is to realize that you don't have to put up with anything that you don't want to put up with. Confident people aren't afraid to bite back and tell people how they really feel. Some people with low self-esteem tend to let people get away with crap and disrespect. If you let people get away with disrespecting, you they'll keep doing it and they won't respect you. Speak up and demand respect. The great thing about being born free is that you're free to just leave or walk away from situations or people that you don't want to deal with. You don't have to put up with anyone's crap or disrespect. You have two feet for a reason. Unless you're a minor you're free to do whatever you want. Well, as long as it's legal. Never think that you're stuck and that you have to put up with someone's disrespect. There's always a way for you not to have to deal with that person. If they're negative and you have no choice but to interact with them, see if you can find a mediator or neutral person to help you out. If someone is being disrespectful or treating you wrong tell them that you won't put up with it anymore. Put your foot down. People know who they can walk over and who they can't. So, if someone is walking all over you, it's because they know you'll put up with it.

There's an orange button on a wall. Out of curiosity, you decide to push it and nothing happens. The next day you push the orange button again and nothing happens. On the third day, you push the orange button out of habit, and the fire alarm goes off. Plus, your boss gets on to you.

1. On the fourth day would you push that button again? _____

2. Nope. Chances are you wouldn't because you can no longer push it without something happening to you.

3. If the alarm didn't go off on the third day would you have pushed it on the fourth day or fifth day? Maybe!

4. If people keep pushing your buttons it's because they know nothing will happen to them. However, if you stand up to them after they push your buttons they'll think twice about pushing it again.

5. From now on will you let people keep pushing your buttons or will you put a stop to it?

_____

Now, let's get back to loving yourself.....

GET TO KNOW YOURSELF

In order to love yourself, you have to get to know yourself and get to the bottom of why you don't love yourself. In order for this guide to help you grab a journal and pen.

Exercise 1: Get to know yourself.

Grab a journal and answer the following questions.

1. What are 3 things that you like about yourself?

    _____

    _____

    _____

2. What is one thing that you're good at?

    _____

3. What are 3 things you dislike about your looks?

4. What are 3 things you hate about your life?

5. Is your past still making you miserable?

6. Do you base your worth on how you look?

7. Have you ever let someone use you or abuse you?

8. Are you a good person?

9. Do you treat yourself right?

10. Do you take care of yourself like you should? _____

11. What's your favorite food? _____

12. What's your favorite movie? _____

13. What are you most afraid of? _____

14. Do you care about what others think of you? _____

15. Have you ever thought about ending your life? Why?

16. Do you have a problem that you think has ruined your life? Explain

17. Are you a good friend? _____

18. What's one thing that makes you happy? _____

19. Do you love anyone? _____

20. Do you have a broken heart? If so, who broke it?

21. Did someone in your past hurt you? If so, who?

22. Are you mad at anyone? Are they in your present life or your past?

23. Do you fight for the things you want in life? _____

24. What do you like to do for fun?

25. Are you happy with your life? _____

26. Do you care about anyone? _____

27. Do you treat yourself the same way that you treat others? _____

28. Do you care about yourself? _____

29. Do you love yourself? If not, why?

30. If you were perfect would you love yourself?

31. Do you constantly put yourself down?

32. Are you doing everything that you should be doing to take care of yourself and your health?

33. Are you fair to yourself or are you mean to yourself?

34. Do you have your own back? _____

35. Do you protect yourself from people who hurt you and disrespect you? _____

36. Are you letting your past mess up your future? _____

37. Do you let people walk all over you or take advantage of you? _____

38. Do you stand up for yourself? _____

39. Are you going to change your life, and start treating yourself better? Or are you going to give up on life, and continue to be mean to yourself?

40. Are you going to start standing up for yourself or are you going to continue to let people walk all over you, disrespect you or use you?

The person in your mirror is counting on you to love and protect them, don't let them down

THE GOOD STUFF

A lot of people with low self-esteem focus on the negative things about themselves more than the positive things. If you constantly focus on the negative things about yourself you'll be miserable, and you'll hate yourself. I mean who would love someone that has nothing but negative things about them? Starting today I want you to stop focusing on the negative things about you. There are good things about you too, and that's what you should be focusing on. Confident people focus on the good things about themselves, and that's why they're happier.

How many of the below things are true about you?

1. You're smart.

2. You have a talent.

3. You're nice

4. You're a good friend

5. You know how to make people laugh

6. You're always there for your friends or family

7. You have won something

8. You have passed a test

9. You graduated from a school

10. Your creative

11. You've helped a stranger

12. You're really good at something

13. You had a job interview, they liked you and they hired you

14. You have forgiven someone for something that was hard to forgive

15. Your heart has been broken, but you still believe in love.

16. Your past was horrible, but you survived it, and you lived to tell about it

17. You've felt like giving up on life, but you kept going

18. People have hurt you, but you're still a nice person

19. Your past was horrible, but you were STRONG enough to get through your past

20. You've donated to charity

21. You've given away clothes or other items to those in need

22. You're a good mom or dad

23. You've volunteered for a charity or other organization

24. You've helped a cause. (Activist, Marched, Marathon, Fundraiser, Petitioned)

25. You've helped someone when they were sick?

26. You do nice things for people without expecting anything in return

27. You've been there for someone when they really needed someone

28. Your career is something that saves lives or helps others in some way

29. You've helped someone when you were in need of help yourself.

30. You've put someone else's needs before your own.

31. You raised someone else's kid

32. You're a good grandmother or grandfather

33. You go out of your way to make people in your life happy.

34. You've been hurt a lot but you don't use that as an excuse to hurt others.

35. You've won an award

36. You've put your life at risk to save someone else's life or to serve your Country.

37. You were strong enough to survive something hurtful or painful.

38. You use your talent to help others.

39. You've created something that you're proud of.

40. You've accomplished a goal or a dream.

41. You've achieved something that was hard to achieve.

How many of the above things applies to you? _____

Are there good things about you? _____

Do you focus on the negative things about you more than the positive things about you?

The above proves that there are good things about you. Things that you should be proud of yourself for. From now on I want you to focus on the good things about you more than the bad things about you. The good things outweigh the bad things, and the good things are more important. The good things about you come from the heart, and the bad things are usually things that are superficial. Don't hate yourself because of your imperfections. Love yourself for the things about you that come from your heart because that's who you really are.

From now on will you FOCUS on the good things about you? _____

You've been there since day one

You're the one person in your life that knows everything about you. I mean everything. You know how hard life has been for you. You know the problems you've faced, you know how many times you've been hurt. You know your flaws, weaknesses, and strengths. You know everything that you've survived and been through. You're the only person that knows every single detail about you. You know how many enemies you have, and how many real friends you have. What you have to understand is that you are the one person in your life that should care about you and embrace you. You know what you've been through in life, you know life hasn't been easy for you, but instead of holding yourself and loving yourself you've turned your back on yourself. Basically, you are your own enemy. Don't you already have enough enemies? What you could really use is a best friend. A best friend that knows every single detail about you, but still loves you. A best friend that knows you've been hurt and that everything in life hasn't been easy for you, but still loves you and hugs you. Realize that turning your back on yourself is like turning your back on someone that has been there for you since day one. Whether you like yourself or not you have to realize that since day one YOU have seen and experienced everything that you've been through firsthand, and you've fought through it. Would you turn your back on a friend that had been there for you since day one? Through your ups and downs and good days and bad days? Nope. You'd thank them, appreciate them, love them, and embrace them. You'd call them your best friend. Well, starting today be your own best friend. Love yourself, be proud of yourself and embrace yourself. Give yourself bear hugs!

From now on will you be your own best friend? _____

Your worth isn't determined by your looks

Society has reached a point where they rank people based on their looks, and they determine a person's worth by their looks. Some magazines even have the hottest people in the world articles. Have you fallen for society's way of determining someone's worth? Do you judge someone's worth by their looks? Do you think someone is better than you because they're more attractive than you? If so, you have fallen for society's false way of determining someone's worth. Realize that just because someone is prettier, smarter or richer than you are it doesn't mean that they are worth more than you. Just because you have more flaws than someone else it doesn't mean that their life is worth more than yours is. Your life is just as important as anyone else's life, and you deserve to be treated just as well as anyone else. Never think that someone else should be treated better than you just because they are more attractive than you are. People that have fallen for society's worth ranking system rank people's worth according to their looks. Then based on this falsely calculated worth they treat people bad or good. Society will rank you based on your looks, but it doesn't mean that you have to accept that rank as a determination of your worth. Your self-worth should be what you think of yourself not what society thinks. In my book 'I Love Me and I Know My Worth' I go over self-worth in more detail.

Starting today I want you to base your self-worth on who you really are inside, and how you want to be treated; NOT by how you look

Realize that you might not be the prettiest, smartest, most popular or richest girl on the planet, but you still deserve to be treated right.

Jill has 2 dogs. One of her dogs has a broken leg, and the other one doesn't.

- *Which dog should she be mean to?* _____

- *Which dog should she hate?* _____

- *Which dog doesn't deserve to be loved?* _____

If you answered 'none' that is the correct answer. In the above, you agreed that both dogs deserved to be loved even though one has a flaw, and one doesn't. Just because one dog has a flaw, and the other one doesn't it doesn't mean that one is worthless. Just because you have more flaws than someone else it doesn't mean that you're worthless or that you deserve to be treated like crap. If you think Jill should be nice to the dog with the flaw, then you should think that people should be nice to you too. Isn't your life just as important as a dog's life? If you think you're worthless because of your flaws, and that you're not good enough to be loved. You might as well say that the dog with the broken leg is worthless because of his flaws, that he should be treated wrong, and that Jill shouldn't love him. It's kind of sad when you think about it, but when you don't love yourself or know your worth you don't care about yourself. You might care about the dog or other people, but you don't care that much about yourself. You don't show yourself the same LOVE that you show others. Also, just because the other dog doesn't have a more noticeable flaw it doesn't mean that it's flawless. Everyone has flaws it's just that some people's flaws are more noticeable than others. The above example proves that everyone should be treated the same regardless of their flaws. Never think that someone else should be treated better than you just because your flaws are more noticeable than theirs are. Always apply your beliefs of what's right and wrong to your own life too.

Should you be treated differently just because you have more flaws than someone else?

_____.

From now on will you demand to be treated with respect just like everyone else because everyone is equal?

_____

Is your life less important than someone that is more popular than you are? _____

Don't punish yourself

Some people that don't love themselves punish themselves by doing things that they know they shouldn't do or by not doing things that they know they should do.

Why? Because this allows them to feel sorry for themselves, and be miserable. I know you're thinking that it's silly that someone would intentionally do things that would make them miserable just to feel sorry for themselves. However, it's a reality and they do it subconsciously. Usually, this type of person is constantly complaining about their life and how miserable they are. Yet they aren't doing anything that could or would take them out of that situation. Or they aren't doing anything that could fix the problem they have even though they are capable of fixing it. Why? Not fixing it allows them to be miserable, and pile that problem or situation onto their list of complaints about why they hate life.

Janet hates her nose so she doesn't take care of her health, hygiene, and other things concerning her body. As a result, her health is deteriorating, her hygiene is suffering, and other things on her body aren't being taken care of properly. On top of that Janet allows men to use her for sex, and take advantage of her. To fix these issues Janet just has to start taking care of her health, her hygiene and taking care of the rest of her body. Also, she can stop letting men take advantage of her and use her. Instead, she just complains about how messed up her life is, and how her health and hygiene aren't as they should be. Why is Janet letting her whole life fall apart even though she has the power to fix most of her issues? It's because it keeps her miserable and it proves something that she believes. What Janet believes is that life sucks, but what she doesn't realize is that she is the one that is making her life worse than what it has to be. Realize that what you believe about life will come true because you will subconsciously do things to make it come true.

1. Are you making your life worse than what it has to be?

2. Do you complain about things that you have the ability and power to change?

3. Do you take care of yourself properly?

4. Do you hold onto people that are making your life miserable?

5. Why aren't you fixing things that you're capable of fixing?

6. Why aren't you taking care of yourself the way that you should?

7. Do you complain about how bad your life is, and then don't do anything about it?

If you aren't taking care of yourself, and you're holding onto people that don't treat you right it's your fault that you're miserable. You have the power to leave the wrong people, and you have the power to take care of yourself. Yet you refuse to do it, and then you complain about it. Life doesn't suck you're just not living life to the fullest. You've given up on life, and then you're complaining about it. Bad things will happen to you in life, but that doesn't mean that you should give up on life. A person who doesn't take care of themselves has stopped caring about themselves. So, they let themselves go, and they let people do all kinds of things to them. Something happened to you that made you stop caring about yourself. Something happened to you that made you give up on life and hate life. Realize that whatever happened to you isn't worth throwing your whole life away for. If you start taking care of yourself, and you give life another chance you'll realize that life isn't bad. It's the people in the world that make life bad sometimes.

People that punish themselves:

1. Don't take care of their health.

2. Don't take care of their hygiene.

3. Give up on their goals and dreams

4. Stay with people who use them, walk all over them or mistreat them.

5. Do things that damage their body.

6. Do things that put their life or health at risk.

7. Do anything that makes them miserable.

8. Complain about problems they are capable of fixing

9. Are you guilty of any of the above? _____

Start spoiling yourself

1. Take yourself out to your favorite restaurant

2. Get a massage and relax

3. Take a trip to somewhere you love.

4. Get a make-over

5. Take care of your hygiene

6. Look the best that you can

7. Clean up your house

8. Chase your goals and dreams.

9. Do things that make you smile?

10. Do something you've never done before

11. Fix things in your life that you're capable of fixing.

12. Give yourself a ton of compliments.

13. Fight for yourself just like you fight for others

14. Do things that will make you proud of yourself

15. Buy yourself something you like

16. Treat yourself like a King or Queen

17. Change your life so you can be a little bit happier

18. Let go of people that aren't good for you.

19. Let go of people that are using you, hurting you or disrespecting you. You don't deserve that

20. Be the person that treats themselves GREAT not good but GREAT

You only have one life. So make it a good life. Don't let bad things in life stop you from enjoying the good things in life.

From now on when you catch yourself complaining about something that you CAN fix remind yourself that you are adding unnecessary problems to your list, and you're punishing yourself. If you can fix it get up and fix it. Stop complaining about something that you have control over.

What are three things that you can do today to take care of yourself just a little bit better?

1.

2.

3.

Will you get those 3 things done today? _____ -

YOU'RE THE BOSS OF YOUR LIFE

Realize that you're the boss of your life, and what you say goes.

- You decide who stays in your life, and who goes.

- You decide what you will, and what you won't put up with.

- You decide what you'll do with your life, and what you won't do.

- You decide whether you'll let something destroy you or whether you'll let it build you into the strongest person you've ever met.

Never let anyone think that they're the boss of your life. You're the boss of it, and make sure they know it. Anyone that doesn't show you love won't be allowed in your life anymore because you only want people that care about you around you.

Read the following paragraph out loud to yourself:

Dear Me: I apologize for not taking care of myself the way that I should, but starting today I will do my best to take care of myself. I don't deserve to be treated wrong or neglected. I'm a nice person and I deserve to be treated nicely, and with respect. From now on I will look out for myself, and protect myself from those who don't care about me. Also, I will fight for myself, and do things that will make me happier. I promise myself these things because I want to be happier, and I want to better my life. Sincerely Me. I love me, and I want the best for me.

Do you pile all of your problems into one pile? _____

DON'T PILE YOUR PROBLEMS INTO ONE PILE

Some people pile all of their woes, and problems into one pile. When something bad happens to them they add it to their past list of things that have happened to them, and then they throw themselves a pity party. Try to keep your bad life events separate. Why? Because piling them all together will make your life seem worse than what it is, and it will send you into a depressed state of mind.

For example; Janet has a flat tire on her way to work, and when she finally arrives to work her boss writes her up. Then Janet sits down at her desk and starts piling all of her life problems into one pile. She piles on her past problems, her ex-boyfriend problems, her chipped nail problems, and any other problem that she can think of. Now, Janet has made her current problem into this big mountain of problems, and she's becoming depressed because of it.

When something bad happens to you stay in the present. Don't dredge up past problems, and add them to the current ones. What happened to Janet at work is bad, but it shouldn't be something that sends her into depression. In fact, piling on problems is why a lot of people get depressed. Deal with your problems separately. Realize that you've already survived most of your past problems, and there's no reason to add them to your new list of problems. Janet had a flat, and a write-up, but the rest of her life is still going well. Also, piling on problems is a way for some people to feel sorry for themselves, and be miserable. They pile on the problems and wallow in their own self-pity. Doing this can become addictive, and some people pile on their problems intentionally just to feel like a victim. I discuss addiction to feeling pain in my book '22 Steps to Moving on After Someone Hurts You'.

Determining your self-worth

People who don't love themselves have low self-worth because as I mentioned earlier they base their worth on the wrong things. Realize that your worth should be based on how you want to be treated.

Exercise 2:

How do you want to be treated? Read the following list and write down every number that describes the type of relationship that you want:

1. I want to be with someone that abuses me.

2. I want to be with someone that uses me or takes advantage of me.

3. I want to be with someone that is verbally abusive and makes fun of me or puts me down?

4. I want to be with someone that is never there for me and doesn't care about me.

5. I want to be with someone that doesn't want to be with me, but still wants everything I've got.

6. I want to be with someone that loves me for who I am flaws and all, and treats me like a Queen or King.

7. I want to be with someone that cheats on me over and over again?

8. I want to be with someone that hits me or beats me.

9. I want to be with someone that acts like I'm not good enough for them.

10. I want to be with someone that uses me for sex, money or other things.

11. I want to be with someone that constantly disrespects me.

What numbers did you choose?

I hope the only number on your paper is the number 6. When you chose number 6 you stated that you want the person you're with to treat you right. Realize that that's what people mean by knowing your worth. Picking number 6 means that you know how you're supposed to be treated, and how you want to be treated. Now, here's the part where people have trouble with. Some people settle for what they don't want, and that's called settling for less. Even though they know they aren't being treated right by someone they still stay with them.

1. Read the above list again, and write down every number that you've settled for before.

2. How many numbers did you pick?

See what I mean? Even though you want to be treated like number 6 you have stayed with people that have treated you like the other numbers. Knowing your worth is different from sticking to your worth. You KNOW you should be treated right, but you aren't sticking to what you believe? From now on if someone isn't treating you like number 6 move on, and don't settle. Don't settle for the other numbers just to keep them in your life or to avoid being alone. Always remember that you decide your worth, and you decide what you will, and won't put up with. Your heart, soul and the real you want to be treated like number 6. Show yourself some love, and only stay with people that treat you like number 6. Protect yourself by leaving people that treat you like the other numbers.

You know what the inner you wants you to settle for, but will you listen to the inner you or not? That's the question. Most people know what they should do, but the real question is "Why aren't they doing it?" Why aren't you sticking to number 6 only? It's because you don't love, and care about yourself the way that you should. If you did you wouldn't allow people to treat you wrong. From now on if Jack or Jill is offering you number 11, and you want number 6 decline their offer instead of changing who you are just to keep them

What's wrong with this sentence? -> " I love you, but I'm going to let people hurt you, abuse you, walk all over you, beat you, and treat you wrong?"

There's no need to analyze the above sentence because you know it doesn't make sense. We both know that isn't what you do when you love someone. That's something you do when you hate someone's guts, and you don't care about them. Actually, most people wouldn't wish the above things on their worst enemy. Yet, they put up with it themselves.

Read the following paragraph out loud to yourself:

Dear me, from now on I will only accept number 6 because I know that I don't deserve to be treated like any other number. Accepting the other numbers is settling for less, and I will no longer settle for less. Sincerely me.

Society

The world can be a cruel place for people that are labeled as unattractive. If a person is considered unattractive some people will treat them wrong just because of how they look. If a person is seen as unattractive people will point out their flaws, make fun of their imperfections, and hate them because of how they look. Unless you've been labeled as unattractive you don't know how it feels to go out in public and have people make rude faces at you because of your flaws. You don't know how it feels for people that you don't even know to stare at you like they hate you or like you disgust them. For people to be so mean to you because of your appearance, and how you were born makes you not want to go out in public. It doesn't stop there. If you're labeled as unattractive you can't even go online without seeing jokes that make fun of people for how they look. You might even be afraid to post a picture of yourself because people might make fun of your picture. To be hated because of your looks is a sad thing. Why can't people be nicer, and more understanding? Society has made joking about someone's look's a form of entertainment. If people were joking day in and day out about your imperfections how would you feel? You wouldn't feel good about it, and after a while, you'd start to hate yourself.

Controlled by Society

Realize that some people are being controlled by society. Society has told them that a person's worth is determined by how they look. Everywhere they go they see images of beautiful people, and they see society praising those people because of how they look. Also, when they go online or out in public they see everyone making fun of those who aren't beautiful, and that the people who make those jokes are seen as 'cool' or 'funny'. Instead of thinking for themselves they go along with society and they praise the beautiful people and put down those who aren't beautiful. When they stare at you with so much hate they are showing you how much power society has over them. Society has them doing exactly what they want them to do, and that is to focus on looks. The beauty industry brings in billions of dollars a year. Women and men spend billions of dollars each year on things that they think will make them more beautiful, and more loved by society. Realize that you don't have to play by society's rules and that you don't have to let society control you like it's controlling them. There's more to life than just looks, and you can focus on those things instead. What else do you have to offer the world besides your looks? Personally, I want to be known for what I've done for the world, and not for how sexy I looked in a dress. I'm not saying that you should feel sorry for the people that make fun of you or stare at you so hatefully. However, the next time they stare at you hatefully look at how much anger they have towards someone they don't know. Where is all that hatred and cruelness coming from? Realize that they are puppets that are being controlled by society. They have been brainwashed to hate or look down upon those who they think are unattractive. They have been told that making jokes online about other's looks is a cool thing, and they've fallen for it. Let society control them, but don't let it control you. Be your own person, and focus on other things in life besides looks. Some of the greatest people that ever lived are found in history books, and they're remembered for what they did for the world, not for how they looked. How do you want to be remembered? Are you letting society control you? Have you looked down on someone just because they weren't attractive as you are? Have you made a joke about someone who wasn't attractive as you are? If so, you are ranking everyone by their looks instead of who they are as a person, and you're determining their worth by how they look. Don't let society control you, and make you treat people wrong just because of how they look. Next time someone stares at you hatefully you don't have to feel sorry for them, but you should realize that they are being controlled by society, and that's really sad.

Do you want to be remembered for how much you've done for the WORLD or for how you look?

I Hate Myself

Why don't you love yourself?

1. Is it because of your flaws? _____

2. Is it because of your past? _____

3. Is it because of what people say about you? _____

4. Do you hate yourself? _____

Before you read the next paragraph write down 3 things you like or love about yourself.

1.

2

3.

Loving yourself doesn't mean that you worship the ground that you walk on or stare at your reflection and think that you're the best thing since sliced bread. It means that you've accepted yourself for who you are flaws and all. Your family members aren't perfect but you still love them right? Right! Therefore, you don't have to be perfect to love yourself. Some people think that self-love means that you have to think you're perfect and that you have to love every inch of you. However, it just means that you've accepted yourself for who you really are. Who you really are is what's inside your heart. It's your character and your personality. If you're a decent person who doesn't intentionally do things to hurt others then you have a nice personality. Realize that everyone has something that they dislike about their appearance. However, people that love themselves don't let that dislike stop them from loving the rest of them. If you hate your nose that doesn't mean that you should hate all of you. What about your personality or your eyes or your other nice features? What about how good of a friend you are? What about your talents? What about your accomplishments? Why do you hate all of you just because of that one thing? Never forget that there are dozens of things about you that you shouldn't hate. How can you say you hate all of those good things about you? No-one hates themselves. In order to hate yourself you'd have to hate everything about yourself, and the majority of people I've talked to were able to give me at least three things that they loved about themselves. Does this sentence make sense --> I hate candy, but I love skittles and snickers? Nope. In order to hate candy, I would have to hate all candy, not just certain kinds. Therefore, in order to hate yourself, you have to hate all of you not just certain parts of you. Therefore, you don't hate yourself you just dislike certain things about yourself. From now on don't say "I hate myself" say "I dislike ___ about myself, but I love everything else about myself." See the difference? When you say you hate yourself you're saying that you hate EVERYTHING about yourself, and you're acting like you don't have anything to love. That's far from the truth. When you say you dislike your nose, but you love everything else about yourself you're being honest, and even though you dislike something about yourself you're still showing yourself love. No-one on the planet hates every single thing about themselves. If you wrote down 3 things you like about yourself that means that you don't hate yourself, you just dislike certain things about you. Realize that happy people focus on the things they love about themselves, not the things they dislike about themselves. Find out what you're good at and use that to change or better your life. Find your best features, and highlight them. Always remember that there are some things that you do love about yourself. If you love some things about yourself you don't hate yourself you just dislike some things, and that's perfectly normal.

Now, do you hate yourself or do you just dislike some things about yourself? _____

To hear someone say they hate themselves is quite sad. Usually, people who say they hate themselves are nice or decent people. So, why would someone who is such a sweetheart hate themselves? Why would anyone hate someone that's nice, and hasn't done anything to deserve so much hate? The answer to that question is even more saddening. Most of them hate themselves because of their flaws and their appearance. Most people want others to look past their looks and get to know their personality. Yet they don't even look past their own looks or flaws. If you know you're a nice, sweet or caring person you need to stop treating yourself wrong. Stop judging yourself by your looks only. It's not fair for you to judge yourself by your cover, and then expect others not to. When you say that you hate yourself because of your appearance you're no different than your enemies or haters. Isn't that what haters and enemies do? Haters and enemies judge you by your looks and ignore all of your good qualities. When you say you hate yourself you're saying that all you care about is looks and that your personality and other great qualities don't matter. Realize that a nice person should be treated nicely. Don't you agree that a nice person shouldn't be hated because of their looks? So, why do you hate yourself? Are you a nice person? Have you done anything to deserve so much hate from yourself? Is it fair to be mean to yourself just because of your appearance? Do you treat yourself right or do you constantly bash yourself and your looks? If someone else treated you the way you treated yourself you'd be mad at them. Yet, you think it's perfectly okay to treat yourself like crap. And the only reason you're treating yourself like crap is because of your appearance. Be nice to yourself for once. Like I said earlier a nice person who hasn't done anything to anyone shouldn't be treated wrong. Be the person that looks past your looks and into your soul. Be the person that points out your good qualities not just your bad qualities. Be the person that doesn't judge themselves or others by their looks only.

"If you hate yourself because of your appearance you're no different than your enemies. In fact, you're worse than them because you know you're a sweet person, but you still treat yourself like crap anyway."

LIFE SUCKS SOMETIMES

Sometimes you'll go through things that a person should never have to go through. Sometimes you'll feel like giving up on everything, and just ending it all. Sometimes you'll feel like screaming because things keep getting worse and worse. However, you have to realize that's just the way life is. In life you're going to get hurt sometimes, you're going to fall sometimes, and you're going to have a lot of bad days. If you think that things have to be perfect in order for you to be happy you'll never be happy. You're unhappy because you think that everything has to be going good and that you have to look a certain way just to be happy. Who made up that rule? If you follow that rule you'll never be happy because you'll always think you need something else or you need to change something in order for you to be happy. Have you ever been in a bad mood, and someone you loved made you smile? Even though you were sad, and things weren't going well you still smiled. Even though they didn't fix what you were mad about you still gave them a smile. Well, even when things are going bad or you hate the way you look you still have to find things to smile about. Most unhappy people focus on miserable things. All day and all night they constantly focus on the negative things in their life, and then they wonder why they're so miserable. Starting today I need you to smile more, laugh more, and go out and enjoy life more. I need you to focus on the good things in life, and I need you to love yourself even though you're not perfect. Who says you have to be perfect just to love yourself? If that were true no-one would love themselves because everyone has flaws. Since you'll never be perfect you have to find a way to love yourself just the way you are.

Life sucks sometimes, but it can also be fun if you want it to be. Bad things will happen to you, but if you keep fighting good things will happen to you too.

1. Have you ever had a fun day?

2. What made that day fun?

3. Life isn't all bad. You can still have fun and enjoy it.

4. What fun things can you do today or this week?

5. What fun things do you do in your spare time?

Today is a new day for you. It's the beginning of a new chapter in your life

Starting today you will no longer see yourself as just a reflection in your mirror. You will see yourself as a person with feelings that wants to be loved and cared for by YOU and others. You will see yourself as a person with dreams that wants you to fight for them. You will see yourself as a person that deserves to be treated right no matter what problems or flaws that you have. You will see yourself as a person that can get their life back on the right track. A person that can love themselves, and a person that can let go of the wrong people. You have to realize that you have more power than you think. You have the power to leave the wrong people. You have the power to change your life. You have the power to love yourself the way you should be loved. However, it's up to you whether you will use that power or not. Once you start using your power to make changes in your life you'll regret not using it sooner because you'll be happier than you've ever been before. You have the power to get back in control of your life. You have the power to kick negative people out of your life. You have the power to accomplish your goals. You have the power to decide whether your life will be a happy life or a miserable life. You can continue living the way that you are now or you can use your power to make your life the best life that it can be. All you have to do is get up, hold your head up, and USE IT. Then keep using it until you get the results you want and need. Once you get up do not I repeat do not sit back down until you've changed your life for the better

5 REASONS PEOPLE DON'T LOVE THEMSELVES

REASON 1: THEIR PARENTS

Not everyone has great parents. Some people have parents that have never shown them love or given them a hug. A child believes that if their own parents don't love them that there is something wrong with them. A mom and dad should love and care for their children, but when they don't the child blames themselves. When the two people that are supposed to care about you don't you begin to question your self-worth? You wonder why they don't love you, and what you can do to make them love you. Parents that don't show their children love distance themselves from their children emotionally, and sometimes physically. This disconnection makes the child feel unwanted, and like they are a disappointment to their parents. They wonder why their dad isn't around or why their mother isn't there for them. They long for a loving family, a family with a mom and dad that cares about them and wants to spend time with them. Some people spend the rest of their life wishing they had a mom and dad like the made-up parents on TV or like the parents their friends have. Parents are a major part in a child's life. A child that knows that their parents love and support them starts life off life on a positive note and has happy memories of their childhood. Because they have parents that love them for who they are they know that they are capable of being loved for who they are flaws and all. A child that can't even get their own parents to love them or support them will be damaged emotionally, and they will have bad memories of their childhood. Also, this emotional damage will reveal itself in their relationship with other people.

The emotional damage caused by their parents reveals itself in future relationships in the following ways:

1. The child who yearned for their parent(s) to love them, but never received their love will yearn for others who don't love them to love them.

2. The child who yearned for attention from a neglectful parent will constantly seek attention from those who don't give them attention

3. The child who yearned for love from an abusive parent, will chase or stay with other abusive people and try to make them love them.

4. The child whose parents made them feel unwanted or unlovable will have self-image and self-worth issues, and stay with people that don't show them love. Why? Because they're used to holding onto people that make them feel unwanted or unlovable. They're used to holding onto people that make them feel worthless or like they're not good enough

5. The child who was sexually abused by a parent or caretaker will have trust issues, intimacy issues or they will be promiscuous or they will allow others to use them sexually.

6. The child who had to do good things in order for their parents or caretaker to show them love/attention will try to buy love from people or they'll give everything they've got to people who don't love them. Why? Because they've learned that doing things for people can earn them love or approval.

How a parent treats their child lays the foundation for how that child will allow others to treat them. Unless there is an intervention or that child learns that the definition of love that they've been taught is wrong they'll continue to be emotionally damaged.

Growing up my life was far from perfect. If I had to describe it in one word, I'd say it was a 'nightmare'. Things got worse and worse before they ever got better, but I never gave up. Oh sure, I thought about giving up several times. At times I felt like taking my own life, and just ending it all. I mean how much can a young girl take? A kid's life should be happy, full of happy memories and stress-free. A kid shouldn't be afraid to go home or afraid of what's going to happen to them. I believe that a kid should have a good home and loving parents, not an unstable home and bad parents. Now, I won't go into detail about my troubled past, but I will tell you this. Learning how to love yourself starts with getting love from your parents and being accepted by your peers. If you've never had parents that hugged you when you fell and skinned your knees. Parents who hugged you and told you that they loved you or parents that told you they were proud of you, it's easy to grow up questioning who you are and what you're worth. I mean what does a kid have to do to get a hug or "I love you?" Well, a kid shouldn't have to do anything but be themselves. They should get hugs and love even when they're acting like a little monster. I mean if your own parents don't love you, of course, you're going to feel worthless, unwanted and unloved. If your own parents treated you like crap you're going to think you're worthless and that you deserve to be treated that way. Every child needs love from their parents or some other grown up to have a healthy self-esteem and self-image. A child learns about love from how they get treated by their parents and other adults. If a child has to earn love from the grownups in their life they will think that love has to be earned. If a child had to do things in order for their parents to approve of them they'll always chase people and try to get approval from them. If a child feels unloved by their parents, they will feel like they're unlovable and that they deserve to be treated like crap. If a child is abused, molested or raped by a parent or someone they trust, chances are they will let someone use them for sex, mistreat them or walk all over them later in life.

REASON 2: THEIR PEERS

Some people grew up with loving parents, but they still don't love themselves because of their peer's opinion of them. Before they arrived at Pre-K or Kindergarten their life was going smoothly. Their parents showered them with love, gave them hugs and kisses, and praised their scribble scrabble drawings. Their mom told them how smart they were or how cute they looked, and they loved themselves. Their parents were a positive part of their life, and their family or neighbors were positive as well. Everyone around them loved them, and treated them nicely or special. Well, except for their siblings from time to time if they had them, but that was something they were used to. However, once they begin school they met people who were negative, and people who judged them because of how they looked. Also, they had teachers who praised them but also gave them bad grades on assignments. They had now entered into the real world, and they were now being judged on looks. If their peers accepted them it confirmed what their parents said about them. If their peers didn't accept them they begin to question if their parents had told them the truth about themselves. A child who believes their peers instead of their parents begins to have low self-esteem. What their peers think about them matters to them more than what their parents think. They think their parents are being nice because they're their parents, and that their friends are telling them the truth. Unless there's an intervention or the kid learns to love themselves they will continue to listen to their peers for the rest of their life. Always look at yourself through your eyes not someone else's eyes. Always think for yourself.

REASON 3: THEIR FLAWS

Some people don't love themselves because of their flaws. They hate how they look or they hate something else about themselves. The only thing they focus on is that flaw, and they are miserable because of that flaw. Just because they have a few flaws they hate themselves. Realize that having flaws doesn't make you unlovable. If someone doesn't accept your flaws they're wrong for you. When you meet the right person they will accept you the way you are. You are more than just your flaws, and the right person will know that. You are more than just your flaws; there are plenty of good things about you, and those are the things you should be focusing on.

REASON 4: THEY HATE THEIR LIFE

They hate their life. Their life is far from what they want it to be, and their life makes them miserable. They need to realize that they're the only person that can change their life. If you're not happy with your life, FIX IT, don't expect someone else to fix it for you.

REASON 5: THEIR PAST

They've been through a lot. Their heart is broken or they're broken. They've been hurt by a lot of people in their past, and they can't get over it. If people are always hurting you and leaving you it can take a toll on your self-esteem and self-worth. People hold onto the past because something made them happy, and they want to feel that same happiness again. Or they hold onto the past because something made them miserable, and it's still making them miserable, and they can't let it go. If you're broken find a way to fix yourself because you can't stay broken forever.

"What can you do to make you happy now? Focus on that!"

The best revenge you can get on the horrible people in your past is to show them that nothing they did or said stopped you from being you.

LOVE AS YOU KNOW IT

Everyone knows the definition of love, but everyone doesn't apply that definition to their life. They know what love is and what love isn't, but they still accept disrespect from people and call it love. Simply because that's what love is to them. If they've only been loved the wrong way they will think that love is supposed to hurt. If no-one has ever loved them for who they are they will think that they have to earn love or prove that they're good enough to be loved. What people put up with in relationships is what they're used to putting up with; it's what they've experienced over and over again in their life. If you're used to being abused by people that love you you'll stay with abusive people. If men molested or raped you as a child you'll probably put up with men that use you for your body or sex. If your mom treated you like crap, chances are you'll put up with women who treat you like crap. If everyone you've ever dated treated you wrong you'll keep dating the wrong type of people because you're used to it, and you'll call it love because that's what love is to you. How they're treating you is far from the real definition of the word love, but it seems real to you because you're used to it, and that's all you know about love. You call how they're treating you love because that's what you've experienced in every relationship you've been in. How they're treating you has become normal to you even if it's far from normal. How they're treating you should turn you off, but you stay with them because you're used to being treated that way. You think it's a normal part of every relationship, and you don't love yourself enough to leave. Some people get abused over and over again by someone, and they think that person loves them simply because that's what they've learned about love through their own experiences. After you've been loved the wrong way you have to get used to being loved the right way. After you've been hurt a lot you get used to the pain and love doesn't feel right without a little bit of pain.

LEARNING FROM WHAT YOU SEE

Some people have learned about love from their parent's relationship. If their dad beat their mom, and she stayed with him they grow up thinking that bad relationships are normal. Not everyone falls into the same patterns as their parents, but most people do it without realizing it. If their mom stayed with their abusive dad and tried to work things out, chances are they will do the same thing if they get used or abused in their own relationships. A healthy relationship isn't perfect, but it should never be abusive. What's your definition of a healthy relationship? If being abused, used, and cheated on is normal to you your definition of a healthy relationship has been tainted by your past experiences. In a healthy relationship, you don't get abused, used or cheated on over and over again. If you think it's a normal part of every relationship your definition of love is far from its true meaning. Once you learn what love really is, and apply it to your life you won't call being hurt over and over again love; you'll call it abuse or getting treated wrong. You'll call it by its real name, and you'll stop giving love a bad name.

THE FIRST STEP IN LOVING YOURSELF

is to learn and understand the real definition of love. Love isn't letting someone use you and walk all over you. Love isn't letting a man that doesn't love you use you for sex. Love isn't letting a man beat you, and give you black eyes. Love isn't letting a man cheat on you over and over again putting you at risk for diseases. Love doesn't make you stay with someone that treats you wrong. Not loving yourself makes you stay with the wrong people. If you loved yourself you wouldn't let someone hurt you and disrespect you over and over again. If you loved yourself you would protect yourself from your enemies, and anyone else that hurts you. When you love yourself you have your own back. Think about the people in your life that you love. Do you have their back? Yes! Do you look out for them and protect them? Yes! Do you get mad at people who hurt them or disrespect them? Yes! Do you want someone to use or abuse someone you love? No, you don't and do you know why? It's because you love them, and that's what you do when you love someone right? Well, if you loved yourself you would get mad at people for hurting you, using you or abusing you. You would get mad at people for walking all over you and treating you like crap. And you would look out for yourself because that's what you do when you love someone. If you don't have your own back you don't love yourself. You can say you love yourself, but actions speak louder than words, and your actions are telling everyone around you how you feel about yourself. How you treat yourself, and how you let others treat you tells the truth about you. If you loved yourself you wouldn't put up with mistreatment. When someone hurts you, blame them for hurting you and blame yourself for putting up with it. If someone keeps hurting you don't ask yourself "Why are they doing this to me?" Ask yourself "Why am I letting them do this to me?" Why are you letting them walk all over you? Oh, it's because you love them and you want them to love you back right? Yes, I know you love them, but do you love yourself or not? If you did you wouldn't be putting up with their crap and letting them treat you like crap. If they loved you they wouldn't be treating you like that. But you'll keep chasing them and staying with them until you love yourself enough to leave.

Realize that a healthy relationship should make you happy not miserable. Realize that a healthy relationship should build you up not tear you down.

THE SECOND STEP

is to realize that the love you experienced in the past wasn't real love. If those people loved you they would still be in your life, and they would have had your back. They would have given you love for free without you having to prove yourself or earn it. They would have cared about you and stood by your side through sickness and in health. Also, if they loved you they would have loved you for who you are flaws and all. If they're not in your life right now or they constantly disrespected you in the past they didn't love you. If you think they loved you your definition of love has been tainted by them and your past. Realize that they were hurting you, betraying you, using you or abusing you not loving you. Once you stop calling how they treated you love you'll stop staying with people who treat you that same way. Until you believe that they didn't love you, you'll constantly stay with people who treat you wrong or you'll constantly chase someone who doesn't want to be with you, and you'll call how they're treating you love.

No-one wants to admit that someone doesn't love them because it hurts too much, and it goes against what they want. So, they make up excuses for how someone treats them.

1. "He loves me, but he just has a strange way of showing it."

2. "She loves me, but he stole her from me."

3. "He loves me, but she seduced him, and she made him cheat on me."

4. "He loves me, but his ex hurt him, and he can't be with me right now."

It's easier to blame someone else or something else than it is to admit that they just don't love you. Once you admit that your past experience with love wasn't real love you'll stop staying with the wrong people, and you'll stop chasing people who don't want to be with you. From now on if someone isn't showing you the real definition of love let them go. Until you realize what love is you're going to accept disrespect and call it love.

Did the person you love show you the real definition of love? _____

If not, don't accept that kind of treatment from anyone else, and don't call that kind of treatment love again.

THE THIRD STEP

is to stop living in the past. All those people in the past shouldn't have hurt you. You didn't deserve to be hurt, and you have every right to be sad or angry. You also have the right to cry over and over again. If you've been hurt you should cry because that's what people do when they're in pain. There's nothing wrong with crying, but after you're done find something to smile about. Realize that the past is over and they can't hurt you anymore. Realize that you can't take back what you've said or done in the past. You've already said or done those things, and you can't take them back so you might as well move on. Realize that you can't change what happened to you in the past. It happened to you, you survived it, and now it's time to move on. You can't change the past, but if you change the present you'll have a better future. Never let what happened to you in the past ruin your future. Never let the person that ruined your past ruin your future. The past is over, you were strong enough to get through it, and now it's time to move on, and focus on your future.

Did you survive your past? _____

Do you still have time to change your life? _____

THE FOURTH STEP

is to never forget how strong you are. If you've been through a lot, and you're still standing you're stronger than you think you are. After all, you've been through, and after all they've done to you you're still alive, and you have survived. Congrats, you made it through hell, but now it's time to go after your goals, and whatever else will make you happy. Be proud of yourself for being strong enough to make it through your past. If you made it through your past you can make it through anything else that happens to you. And if anyone tries to bring you down tell them to get in line with the people that have already tried, and failed because you are a survivor.

"A strong person can go through hell and still find a way to be happy."

Were you strong enough to survive ALL of the things that has happened to you? _____

Treat yourself right

Do you know how it feels to look in the mirror, and not like what you see? Do you know how it feels to wish that you could be someone else? Someone that is prettier or better off than you? If you could only be them your life would be so much better, and you'd finally love yourself. If you could just get rid of your flaws you'd be someone that you could love. Yet every day you wake up and you're still you. You're still the person that you despise and disapprove of. How can you love yourself when you hate so much about yourself? How can you love yourself when you have so many flaws or problems? Well, you have to understand that you're telling yourself the meanest thing a person could ever tell another person. You're telling yourself that you can't love someone that looks like you, and that you're unlovable because of how you look. Would you tell your best friend that you can't love them because of how they look? Imagine the pain in their eyes, and the sadness in their face if you told them these words "Dear friend, I can't love you because you have too many flaws. Dear friend, I hate you because of how you look." Those words are so heartbreaking, and you'd never say that to your friends or family. Why would you be so mean to them because of how they look? Why would you tell them that you hate them because of their flaws? To say those words to a loved one would be cruel, and yet every time you look into a mirror you say those words to yourself. Realize that whether those words are said to a friend or said to yourself that it's still cruel and heartbreaking. To look into the mirror, and tell the person staring back at you that you don't love them. To tell them that you hate them because of how they look. To tell them that their flaws make them unlovable is beyond cruel. Yet day in and day out you continue to crush your own soul. Don't you see the pain in your own eyes, and the sadness in your own face when you tell yourself these things? Understand that there's more to life than just looks, and if you don't limit yourself there's an unlimited amount of things that you can do with your life.

THE FIFTH STEP

is to love yourself flaws and all. We all have stuff we hate or dislike about ourselves, but we should never let those things make us hate everything else about ourselves. I mean there are plenty of good things about you too, and that's what you should be focusing on. Focus on how smart you are, how talented you are at something, how good of a mom or dad you are. How good of a friend you are, how nice you are, how good you are at cooking or learning new things. There are so many good things about you so never forget that. Never let a few flaws make you hate everything else about yourself. The people that love you won't care about your flaws anyway, and if someone doesn't like you because of your flaws they're superficial and judgmental. And who needs a superficial person in their life anyway? Always remember that there's more to you than just your looks, and the people that love you won't care about your flaws.

The person in your mirror bashes you more than anyone else does. You're supposed to love the person in your mirror not hate them. What has the person in your mirror done to you for you to bash them so much? The person in your mirror wants you to love them for who they are flaws and all. The person in your mirror wants you to love them just like you love everyone else. They want you to have their back, they want you to give them compliments, they want you to protect them, and they want you to do whatever it takes to make them happy. The person in your mirror wants you to stop judging them and putting them down. They just want to live life and be happy. Will you give them a chance to be happy? Will you do whatever it takes to make them happy or will you give up on them? Can you tell the person in your mirror some good things about them? Can you stop putting them down so much? The person in your mirror hasn't done anything to deserve your harsh words or put downs. They just want to be loved by you, flaws and all. For who they are, and not for who you want them to be. The person in your mirror knows they're not perfect, but they still want you to accept them. Does the person in your mirror have to be someone else just for you to like them? You owe the person in your mirror an apology for the way you've treated them, and after you apologize you need to start treating them right; because when you love someone you treat them right.

From now I want you to give yourself 3 compliments every time you look in the mirror. I want you to stop putting yourself down because it's not fair to you. Never put yourself down or bash yourself. It's not right when other people bash you, and it's not right when you bash yourself. If you're constantly bashing your own looks you are your own bully, and you're being cruel to yourself. Treat yourself the same way that you want others to treat you. Starting today you need to start giving yourself some compliments and stop bullying yourself. Show yourself some freaking love. Stop treating yourself like crap. Before we go to step 6, tell me 3 good things about you. Don't go to step 6 until you do. Also, every time you catch yourself bashing yourself, I want you to give yourself a compliment. Replace all your put downs with compliments.

From now on will you give yourself MORE compliments or more put downs?

_____

Has anyone ever made fun of you? _____

When someone makes fun of you I want you to realize that what they're saying about you isn't about you. They could care less about your flaws because your flaw doesn't affect them in any way. When they make fun of you, it's for one of the following reasons.

1. **They are jealous of you** - They're jealous of your looks, success, relationship, wealth, popularity or anything else that you have that they don't have.

2. **Your flaws make them feel better about their own flaws** - They make fun of people who have more flaws than they have so they can feel better about their own flaws.

3. **They're bitter-** They're hurting inside or they're angry and they want someone to take their anger out on.

4. **For attention or Popularity** -This person bashes you or makes fun of you for attention or popularity. They usually do this in front of a group of people for laughs or attention.

All of the above reasons have nothing to do with you; they're just making fun of you for their own selfish reasons. Next time they make fun of you just remember that it's not about you. If they're around a group of people or it's in public just know they're doing it for attention. If you're successful or popular they might make fun of you out of jealousy. If the person acts like they're angry or mad at you, they're just taking their anger out on you, and something else is going on in their life. Once you realize that it's not about you, it will be easier to deal with people who bash you. Just ignore them because their opinion can't ruin your life or happiness unless you let it. Never let someone else's opinions of you make you hate yourself. Just focus on the people that love you and care about you. Haters and enemies shouldn't control you or your emotions.

Raining on your own parade

When you look into the mirror or examine your life negative thoughts will pop into your head. These thoughts will try to ruin your day or bring you down. No matter how happy a person is they will have negative thoughts pop into their head occasionally. These thoughts are your way of keeping yourself from being happy. Sometimes we're so used to being unhappy that we can't enjoy the happy moments when they come. So, we find things about ourselves or our life that we can bash that will bring us back to feeling unhappy. Try to enjoy the happy moments without raining on your own parade. Let yourself celebrate the present without letting past memories or negative thoughts ruin the celebration.

From now on when these negative thoughts pop into your head replace it with these positive thoughts.

1. **I hate myself** – I dislike some things about myself, but I'm still good enough to be loved.

2. **I hate my flaws** – I wish I didn't have this flaw, but there are other things about myself that I like.

3. **I hate life** – I dislike some things about life, but I have had happy days, and I will have happy days again.

4. **I hate the way I look** –Even though I'm not 100 % happy with my looks, I'm still a great person, and I can still do great things with my life.

5. **I hate my life** - I hate how my life is right now, but I'm going to do whatever I can to fix it. Then once I fix it I'll be happier.

6. **I hate my flaws** – Everyone has flaws, so it's normal to have flaws. Perfect people don't exist.

7. **I hate myself** – Okay me, be nice to yourself. Be your own best friend, not your own worst enemy

8. **I hate myself** – Hey me, stop treating yourself like that. You have good things about you too. Let's focus on those things instead.

9. **I hate my life** – I hate how my life is. So, what am I going to do to change it? I know, I can go after what makes me happy, and stop procrastinating. No more excuses it's time for me to do better.

10. **I hate that flaw** - I hate that flaw, but I'm not going to let that flaw ruin my whole life. I'm not going to let my flaws hold me back in life. I have more to offer the world than just my looks. I don't have to be the prettiest or most handsome person in the world to accomplish my goals. Who I am can't be seen with the eyes. Who I am can only be seen by getting to know me. Once you get to know me you'll realize that I'm a great person.

Basically, every time you have a negative thought follow it up with a positive one. Never let the negative thoughts have the last word.

THE SIXTH STEP

is to focus on the things you're good at. Stop focusing on the things you can't do, and start focusing on the things you can do. There are plenty of good things you can do with your life if you fight and never give up. If you've fallen find a way to get back up. If you don't know where to start right down a list of things you want to accomplish and start off with something small and work your way up to the bigger things. In order to love yourself, you have to go after your goals and dreams. When you were a kid you wanted to be something and the little kid inside of you still wants to be something. Get up and do the things you've always wanted to do. The only person stopping you from achieving your goals is you and your excuses. Every excuse you make pushes you further away from your goals. It's never too late to go back to school. It's never too late to go after your dream job and it's never too late to do a hobby or something else you've wanted to do. It's not too late until you're dead and if you're reading this you're not dead yet. You can sit around and feel bad for yourself or you can get up and try to better yourself. Your past might be dark, but you can still have a bright future. Just because you had a bad beginning it doesn't mean that you can't have a happy ending. The best stories aren't about people with a nice past, they're about people who survived a bad past, lived their dreams and had a happy ending.

THE SEVENTH STEP

Are you afraid to do things because you're afraid that people will make fun of you? _____

is to live without the fear of being judged. Most people are afraid of being judged. So, they live their life according to how society and their peers expect them to. They let society tell them how to look, how to dress and how to live their life, and do you know why they do it? It's because they are afraid that society will judge them, talk about them or make fun of them if they don't. They're letting their enemies and society control them. They're afraid to try something because they don't want people to see them fail. They're afraid to dress a certain way because they're afraid that people will judge them. They're afraid to love who they want to love because they're afraid of being judged. In order to love your life, you have to live your life for you and set yourself free from society's rules. Live your life the way you want to live it. If your enemies want to judge you and watch you; let them watch you chase your goals. Let them watch you chase your dreams, and let them watch you be happy. Give them front row seats, and let them eat popcorn while they watch you enjoy your life. If they don't like you, the way you look or how you live your life that's their problem, not yours. Your life will still go on with or without them. Don't let the fear of being judged hold you back or stop you from doing what you want to do with your life.

From now on will you let your FEAR of being judged stop you from doing what you want to do in life?

_____

THE EIGHTH STEP

is to stop giving your enemies control over you, your life and your emotions. If your enemy's words have the power to make you hate yourself you're letting them control you. If your enemy's opinions has the power to stop you from doing something you're letting them control your life. Never give an enemy that much power over you. Never let an enemy ruin your day, there are more important things that you should be focusing on. If you take away the power that your enemies have over you, they won't be able to hurt you. The only weapons your enemies can use against you are the ones that you let get to you.

If someone is trying to make you mad or they're attacking you verbally stay calm, and stay in control of yourself, and your emotions. Don't let their words control you or mess up your day. Your enemies want you to be mad and unhappy. They want to mess up your day, and they want to control you. Stay calm, and just fix the problem as best you can. Always be the calmest person in the argument. When you let their words make you angry or out of control you're letting them control you. When you catch yourself getting mad at someone's words or actions remember that you're letting them control you, and then find a way to get back in control of yourself. Once you get back in control of your emotions a weight will lift off of your shoulders, and you'll no longer be upset because of what they've said or done. Always use logic instead of emotions to deal with your problems. When you use logic you just deal with the problem, and you leave the emotions out of it. When you use emotions to fix your problems you let the problem control you, your emotions, and your reactions. If the other person is really mad at you or they're really hostile excuse yourself from the conversation or room. Tell them that you will talk to them when they have calmed down. Always stay in control of the argument. Never let an argument make you out of control or angry. Control your problems don't let your problems control you. To win against an enemy do the opposite of what they expect you to do. If they're trying to make you mad, stay happy. If they want your attention, ignore them. Never let an enemy's problem become your problem. Just because they're mad about something it doesn't mean that you have to be mad too. Just because they hate you it doesn't mean that you have to hate yourself. If your haters or enemies have a problem with you that's their problem, not yours. You have better things to do, and more important people to focus on.

You have power over your haters.

A hater's job is to make you hate yourself. So, you shouldn't be surprised at the things they say or do. When you're surrounded by enemies you're going to get bashed, judged, and talked about. That's life. Everyone gets judged so you're not alone. Haters will say anything to bring you down, and they'll do anything to make you miserable. However, realize that nothing they do or say can bring you down unless you let it. That's right! You have the power to decide whether it brings you down or not. If they insult you, it's up to you whether that insult brings you down or not. That insult doesn't have power until you give it power. If I were you I wouldn't give their words any power. Who cares what they say? At the end of the day, it's your life, and whether they like you or not you're still going to be alive. Think about all the insults people have thrown at you before. Those insults might have hurt you temporarily, but it didn't kill you. It didn't kill you because it's just words, and words don't have power unless you give it power. Next time someone throws an insult at you, remind yourself that they're trying to bring you down to their level. They're miserable so they want you to be miserable too. Let their insults go in one ear and out the other ear, and try your best not to let their words have power over you.

A haters job is to HATE you

What is wrong with this sentence? -->"I hate myself because of what my enemies say about me"

They hate themselves because of what their ENEMIES say about them. A person should expect their enemies to say negative things about them because that's what enemies do. Saying hateful, negative things about you makes them your enemy. Secondly, why do your enemies have so much power over you? If an enemy's words can make you hate yourself, you've given their words too much power. An enemy's job is to bring you down by any means necessary. If what they're saying about you is bringing you down, then they are doing their job. So, the question is why are you listening to your enemy's opinion of you? That's like listening to the opposite team during a match. That's like listening to someone that is trying to destroy you. That's like being in a war and listening to your opponent's advice. Okay, you get the point. Well, it doesn't make sense. Stop listening to your enemies because nothing they say or do is to benefit you. They're only trying to bring you down. Do you hate yourself because of what your ENEMIES say about you? Why are you giving your enemies that much power over you? Should you listen to someone that is trying to bring you down? Stop listening to them. Show them that you're the boss of your life, and their opinions of you aren't going to ruin your life. Realize that if you keep listening to your enemies they're going to bring you down, and they're going to win. Are you going to control your life or are you going to let your ENEMY control it? It's your life, and you get to decide who controls it.

Realize that your enemy's job is to make you miserable. They are constantly looking for a way to bring you down and make you miserable. So, they're going to say or do anything to bring you down. Your haters will point out your flaws and throw them in your face every day. Your enemies will dig up your past just to ruin your present life. A hater's job is to hate you. To win against your enemies you can't let anything they do or say stop you from being you. The minute you do is the minute they've won. The minute you do is the minute they are controlling you, your self-worth, your self-esteem and everything else in your life. Never give your enemies that much power over you.

THE NINTH STEP

is to not let anyone tell you who you are. People will think things about you, but what matters is what you believe. People will always talk about you, but their opinions shouldn't affect how you feel about yourself. Never put yourself down because of someone else's opinion of you. Think for yourself. The only thing they can do is talk or laugh, but they can't control your life or stop you from being happy unless you let them. Never let anyone tell you who you are, hold your head up high, look them in the eyes, and tell them who you are. People will always talk about you, but they have problems too, they're just focusing on yours instead of their own. If they keep focusing on your life they have no life.

Who you really are

Your body is just a shell for your soul. Who you really are can't be seen by looking in the mirror it has to be seen by getting to know you. Sure there are some people who will judge you based on the way that you look, but those people aren't the type of people that you need in your life. The people that take the time to get to know the real you are the people that deserve a place in your life. If a beautiful person never spoke one word the only thing you'd know about them were that they were beautiful, but you wouldn't know who they really were until you got to know them. No matter how you look people don't know you unless they get to know you. Therefore, a person who judges you by just your looks doesn't know anything about you, and their opinion of you shouldn't matter to you. For if they had gotten to know you before they judged you or assumed things about you because of your looks they'd realize that you're a nice person. For them to be so cruel or mean to you without knowing anything about you reveals a lot about them and their character. When someone judges your looks realize that they are judging something that is a part of who you are, but it's not all that you are. You're more than just your looks, and if they just get to know you they'd know that. If they don't want to get to know you just because of how you look they aren't the type of person that you should want to get to know. Why do you want to get to know someone that hates you because of how you look? Why do you care about their opinion of you when they don't even know anything about you? From now on if someone doesn't get to know you realize that they are basing their opinion of you on your looks, and not who you really are.

From now on will you define yourself or will you let others define you? _____

Define yourself below. Who are you? What are you worth?

_____

_____

_____

_____

_____

_____

_____

THE TENTH STEP

is to stop being jealous of others. If you're jealous of someone else's life that means you're unhappy with your own life. Start doing things to make your life better so you can be happy. Don't be jealous of them, just use them for inspiration, and get tips from them.

1. What about them makes you jealous?

2. Why does it make you jealous?

3. Are you jealous because they have something that you want?

4. How can you fix your life so you can be happy with it?

From now on when you catch yourself getting jealous ask yourself "What can I do to fix my life so I won't be jealous of their life".

Someone will always be prettier, smarter or richer than you, but it doesn't mean that they are better than you. So, never put yourself down or act like you're beneath them. When you're really jealous of someone you tend to put them above you and act like you're beneath them. Just because they have something that you don't have it doesn't mean that you're beneath them. We're all human, and we're all equal. Their life isn't more important than your life. You're just as special as they are. You just have to focus on the positive things about yourself instead of the negatives. Most people are famous because they've found something they're good at, and they've used that skill or talent to change their life or make their dreams come true. Start focusing on the good things about you, and find ways to use those things to change your life or make your dreams come true. Once you start focusing on the positive things in your life you'll be happier, and your life will change for the better. Focusing on negative things makes you miserable, and unhappy.

From now on will you focus on your life or their life? _____

THE ELEVENTH STEP

is to be honest with yourself 24/7. Don't lie to yourself just to make yourself feel better. Deal with what's really happening to you. Deal with how they're really treating you. Be honest with yourself and your feelings. How do you really feel about your life and the decisions you've made? How do you really feel about the way they're treating you? Are you happy with your life or not? Do you like the way they treat you or not? Always give yourself the real answer so you can deal with what's really happening to you. If you lie to yourself nothing will change, and you'll be living a lie. People lie to themselves to make themselves feel better, and to avoid dealing with the truth. The truth hurts, and they can't handle it. The truth hurts, but the sooner you accept it the sooner you can deal with it and move on. Lying to yourself hurts you, and it keeps you in situations or relationships that you shouldn't be in. If you start telling yourself the truth your life will be so much better.

"You can accept the truth now or later, but you can't run from it forever"

"I'd rather hear the bitter truth than the sugar coated lie"

"Tell yourself the bitter truth, not the sugar coated lie"

THE TWELFTH STEP

is to realize that you can't change everything, and you can't fix everything. However, just because you can't change it, it doesn't mean that you should let it ruin your whole life. Never let a few bad things ruin everything else in your life. There are plenty of other things you can change or fix so focus on those things. If you can't fix it try not to worry about it just focus on something that you can fix. Don't give up on everything in life just because you can't fix that one thing.

Is that one thing worth throwing your whole life away for?

Don't be so hard on yourself. Give yourself a chance to enjoy life. Everything in life can't be fixed, but you can still enjoy the little things in life, and you can still go after your dreams. Never let anything or anyone take away your chance at happiness. Life's too short to let one thing ruin everything. You've fought too hard, and you've come too far to just give up on everything because of that one thing.

A wise person focuses on the 100 things they can fix not the 1 thing that they can't fix.

What's wrong with this scenario? -> "Janet hates herself and her life. She can't get over her past, she hates her appearance, and she has a problem that she can't fix. She's smart with a lot of potential, but she has given up on her goals and other things. All she ever thinks about is that problem that she can't fix. She thinks that problem has ruined her life, and she believes she'll never be happy because of it.

Janet is letting one problem ruin everything else in her life. Does that make sense? Janet is letting her flaws stop her from chasing her goals. Does that make sense?

Stop letting problems, flaws, and other issues control your whole life. You have to learn how to separate your life into sections. One section should be the things that you CAN fix, and the other section should be things that you CAN'T fix. Happy people focus on the CAN fix section of their life, and miserable people focus on the CAN'T fix section of their life. What section are you focusing on? If you focus on the CAN'T section you won't get anything done because those things can't be changed. If you focus on the can section you'll get thousands of things done because those are things you can change. I don't want to hear a list of things you can't do, I want to hear a list of things you can do because that's the list that can change your life. Janet can't fix that one problem, but if she uses her smarts she can fix a thousand other things in her life. Are you going to continue to let something you can't change or fix destroy your whole life? Or are you going to start focusing on the things you can fix? Don't let your potential go to waste. We all have problems that we can't change or fix. However, some people accept it and move on to other things that they can fix, and others just give up on everything. You're more than just that problem or flaw. There are other things about you that you can use to better your life or change it. Or there are other things you can do even though you have that problem. Find a way to live with that problem instead of letting that problem stop you from living. I have flaws and problems, but I'm not going to let those things stop me from accomplishing the things I want in life. Don't let it stop you either. Always remember that you have other things to offer the world besides looks or other superficial things.

THE THIRTEENTH STEP

is to stop focusing on the bad things in your life. There are some things that you'll never get over, but if you keep fighting and you keep your head up there's nothing that you can't get through. If you keep fighting good things will happen to you too. Never forget that there are good things about you, and that good things can happen to you. Also, realize that the world is full of good things; it's the people in the world that make it bad sometimes. There are plenty of good things, but you'll never find them until you let go of the bad things. If you keep focusing on the bad things in your life your life will seem worse than what it is. Happy people focus on the good things in their life, and miserable people focus on the bad things in their life.

THE FOURTEENTH STEP

is to never give up on yourself. No matter how hard things get keep fighting until you make it through it. If you give it all of your strength, you'll get through it. Never give up, if you push yourself and give it your all you'll get it done. Realize that if you give up things won't change and you'll be stuck where you're at now. If you don't like how your life is or where you're at in life keep fighting until you get to where you want to be. Your future and your kid's future depend on you and what you do with your life. If you hate being at the bottom keep fighting until you get to the top. Promise yourself that you will better your life for you, your future family and your future.

If you want to change your life read the following sentences OUT LOUD:

STARTING RIGHT NOW I PROMISE MYSELF THAT I WILL DO WHATEVER IT TAKES TO REACH MY GOALS.

1. **I PROMISE MYSELF THAT I WILL STOP MAKING EXCUSES FOR WHY I CAN'T CHANGE MY LIFE.**

2. **I PROMISE MYSELF THAT I WILL GIVE LIFE MY ALL AND PUSH MYSELF UNTIL I GET THINGS DONE.**

3. **I PROMISE MYSELF THAT I WILL TAKE CARE OF MYSELF.**

4. **I PROMISE MYSELF THAT I WON'T EVER GIVE UP ON MYSELF.**

5. **I PROMISE MYSELF THESE THINGS BECAUSE I DESERVE TO BE HAPPY.**

6. **I PROMISE MYSELF THESE THINGS BECAUSE I WANT TO CHANGE MY LIFE.**

7. **I PROMISE MYSELF THESE THINGS BECAUSE I WANT TO BE PROUD OF MYSELF.**

8. **I PROMISE MYSELF THESE THINGS BECAUSE I DON'T WANT MYSELF OR MY FAMILY TO STRUGGLE.**

9. **I PROMISE MYSELF THESE THINGS BECAUSE I LOVE MYSELF AND I WANT MYSELF TO BE HAPPY.**

10. **I PROMISE MYSELF THAT I WON'T BREAK MY OWN PROMISES.**

I WON'T BREAK THESE PROMISES BECAUSE I'M TIRED OF THE WAY MY LIFE IS AND I'M READY TO CHANGE IT.

SIGNED BY ME _____ DATE _____

"Next time you think you can't do it, push yourself and give it your all, and you'll prove yourself wrong."

"If you push yourself you'll realize that you can get further than you think you can and you'll realize that you're stronger than you think you are"

"When was the last time you gave something your all? If you can give them your all you should be willing to do the same for yourself."

"When you love someone you don't give up on them. Even when they fall, fail or make mistakes you still love them, and you stick by their side. Start loving yourself, and you won't give up on yourself again"

THE FIFTEENTH STEP

is to realize that you deserve to be loved. Not for what you can do for someone, but for who you really are. If you're a good person you deserve to be treated well. You're something so don't let them treat you like your nothing. Never let anyone walk all over you because you haven't done anything to deserve that. Too many good people are putting up with things they don't deserve. They're so sweet, but they're wasting all of their time on someone who doesn't appreciate them or on someone that's wrong for them. You might love the person that's using you, cheating on you or hitting you, but if they're not treating you right you should leave because you deserve to be loved too. Why should they get all of your love when they're not giving you anything but heartbreak and misery? You're a somebody so don't let them treat you like you're a nobody.

THE SIXTEENTH STEP

is to accept yourself. Realize that you'll never be perfect, and your life will never be perfect, but that's perfectly fine. Being imperfect is normal and everybody on planet earth is imperfect. Nobody's perfect and everyone makes mistakes so give yourself a break. That's right! Give yourself a freaking break. Stop putting yourself down and start showing yourself some love. If you can love everyone else flaws and all why can't you love yourself? If you can love them why can't you love yourself flaws and all? Start showing yourself the same love you show them. Show yourself unconditional love, love that loves you for who you are. Accept that you'll never be perfect. The people that love you don't care about your flaws or problems they just love you for who are you. Also, think about the people that you love. Even though they have flaws and problems you still love them right? Yes, you do because that's what real love is. When you love yourself you overlook your flaws and you love yourself for who you are inside. When I look at my loved ones their flaws don't matter, I just love them for who they are and what they mean to me. When you meet someone that really loves you they'll overlook your flaws and love you for who you are. If someone judges you or hates you because of your flaws they don't belong in your life, and their opinions shouldn't affect you in any way. Focus on the people that love you because they are the ones that matter. Some people are so busy worrying about who doesn't love them that they forget to make time for the people that do love them. Always remember that you don't have to be perfect to be happy.

THE SEVENTEENTH STEP

is stop taking rejections personally. Some people will hate you for no reason, and others will hate you for a stupid reason. If they don't like you that's their problem, not yours. Your life will go on with or without them. Also, some people will reject you, and act like you're not good enough. Rejection hurts because people take it personally. When someone rejects them they think that they're not good enough or that something must be wrong with them. When someone rejects you it doesn't mean that something is wrong with you or that you're not good enough it means that they're wrong for you. When you find the right person they won't reject you, and they won't act like you're not good enough. When someone rejects you say good riddance because they're wasting your time. Next time you get rejected by someone don't take it personally just take it as a sign that they're not the one and move on. When they reject you don't chase them and try to prove yourself to them and don't try to make them love you. Just move on. Never give up on love because the right person for you is still waiting for you. Not everyone will like you, but you should always like yourself. What others think of you doesn't matter, but what you think of yourself does matter.

Being rejected hurts, but realize that rejection is a sign that you're trying to be with someone that you're not meant to be with.

THE EIGHTEENTH STEP

is to let go of anger. To love yourself you have to get rid of the bitterness in your life. Your past might be messed up, but you can't stay broken forever, find a way to fix yourself. Whoever hurt you in the past is stuck in your past, and they can't hurt you anymore. If you're still bitter because of what they did to you you're letting them control your emotions. You might not get over what they did to you, but you can't let what they did to you ruin your whole life. To be happy, you have to be strong and find a way to move on. The person you're mad at might have moved on, and they're not even thinking about you. So, your anger and bitterness isn't hurting them, it's hurting you. When you let go of the anger you have towards them the bitterness will disappear from your life. Also, if you let go of the anger you'll stop living in the past, and they won't have power over your emotions anymore. Take your life back from them, and stop letting them make you bitter and angry. Stop letting them control your life and your emotions. Stop letting them ruin your present life and your future. Start living again. Start chasing your goals and dreams, and other things that will make you happy. They messed up your past, but don't I repeat don't let them mess up your future. You can be strong and you can get through this. Stop focusing on past memories and go out and create new memories. You didn't deserve what they did to you, but you do deserve to be happy. So, wipe that frown off your face and go after what will make you happy. Keep fighting, and don't let them win. Never let them win! You can defeat your enemies.

THE NINETEENTH STEP

is to smile. Smile because you're still alive. Smile because you were strong enough to make it through your past. Smile because you still have your whole future ahead of you. Smile because you defeated your past enemies. Smile because you're a nice person and you deserve to be happy. Smile because things will get better. Smile because you have the power to smile, to be happy and to go after your goals and dreams. Smile because you want to, and don't let anyone take away your smile. If you can still smile after all you've been through you're a warrior and a survivor. Be proud of yourself.

THE TWENTIETH STEP

is to live your life. Every day do something that will make you smile, and better your life. Go out and do new things. Do the things you've always wanted to do. Go places you've never been. Look up at the stars, watch the sunrise, feel the wind blow against your face. Just live your life and be happy, happy, and happy. Love yourself, take care of yourself, and be yourself. Don't be afraid to try new and exciting things. If you're always bored it's because you're always sticking to your same routine. Change things up a bit, and keep your life interesting. When you're always chasing your goals, and trying new things you don't get bored. Never get too comfortable, there's always something that you should be doing or working on to better yourself or your life.

The TWENTY-FIRST STEP

is to surround yourself with people that love you. If you surround yourself with people that make you feel worthless, you'll be miserable. If you surround yourself with people who act like you're not good enough, you'll feel like you're not good enough. In order to love yourself, you have to get rid of everyone and everything that makes you miserable. Replace negative things in your life with positive things. The less stress you have in your life the happier you'll be. Get rid of people that put you down or try to bring you down.

THE TWENTY-SECOND STEP

is to face your problems. Don't run from your problems, fix them. If your life is a mess, clean it up. Most problems can be fixed; you just have to find a way to fix them. If a problem can't be fixed move on to a problem that can be fixed. Don't give up on everything in your life because of a few problems. A person with an unfixable problem can still be happy. You might not be able to fix 5 of your problems, but you can definitely fix 100 of them. So, get busy.

What are five problems in your life that you can fix?

1. _____

2. _____

3. _____

4. _____

5. _____

How and when will you fix the above?

THE TWENTY-THIRD STEP

is to stop making excuses to get out of things. If it's something that can change your life and make you happier do it. Every excuse you make pushes you further away from your goals. Making an excuse to get out of doing something that could better your life hurts you and your future. Most people make excuses to get out of hard work. Deep down inside they don't think they can do it or they think it's too hard, so they make up an excuse to get out of it. Never tell yourself that you can't do something. If you try it you might do better than you think you can. It's okay to feel sorry for yourself sometimes, but realize that feeling sorry for yourself won't change anything. If you want something to change you have to do something about it.

THE TWENTY-FOURTH STEP

is to believe in yourself. Realize that you can do anything that you want to do. Believe that you will have a great future, and you will reach your goals. Once you believe something, and you put effort into it, you'll accomplish it. Your attitude should be that there is nothing you can't do. Never tell yourself that you can't do something. If you haven't tried it you have no idea what you can do. If you push yourself and give it your all you'll be surprised at how far you can go. Never forget how strong you are and never forget all the things you've accomplished in the past. Stop focusing on your failures, and just focus on your accomplishments. Never think that you're not good enough. You're always good enough for the people that love you, and you can be anything you want to be in life if you fight, and never give up. If someone acts like you're not good enough they're the wrong person for you. Replace negative thoughts with positive thoughts. Next time you catch yourself saying that you can't do it, you don't have the time or it will be too hard. Realize that you are being negative, and you're holding yourself back. Then change those negative statements into positive statements. Next time "I can't do it" pops into your head believe in yourself and tell yourself that you can do it. It might be hard to accomplish, but you can do it. If you think something is too hard for you, remind yourself that you can do it, but it will just take a little longer to get it done. You have to believe in yourself, and stop telling yourself that you can't do things. You can do it if you try, and never give up. Stop being so mean to yourself, and give yourself a chance to win. Give yourself a chance to succeed, and be happy. Stop holding yourself back, and start pushing yourself towards your dreams.

When you were a kid and someone asked you what you wanted to be you answered it with so much enthusiasm, and you believed that you could be anything you wanted to be. You believed that you were great, and you believed that your dreams would come true. Well, if you're reading this book and you've given up on yourself or your goals, you have also stopped believing in yourself. That feeling you had that you could be anything has been replaced with a bunch of "I cant's, it's too hard's, I'm not good enoughs, I don't care anymore's, I give ups and a bunch of other excuses. You have stopped believing in your greatness, and how great your future can be. You have stopped caring about yourself and your future, but what made you stop caring? What made you give up on your future, and stop believing in yourself?

1. Maybe you fell, and you think you can't get back up.

2. Maybe someone hurt you, and you can't get over what they did to you

3. Maybe you don't care about your life, and you'd rather not be alive

4. Maybe you're going through something that you think you can't get through.

5. Maybe you don't think you're smart enough or good enough to accomplish your goal anymore

6. Maybe you're afraid to go after your dreams because you think you'll fail

7. Maybe you're afraid that people will judge you

8. Maybe you've been through a lot and you're hurting inside.

9. Maybe you're going through dozens of these maybes and it's too much for you to handle.

No matter what your reason is, you are letting that reason ruin your life. You are letting that reason get in the way of your happiness, and you're letting it stop you from going after your goals or dreams. Is that reason worth your whole life? Are you going to give up on your whole life because of that reason? Your life is more important than that reason. From now on I want you to replace the reasons you think you can't do something with the reasons why you have to do it. Instead of saying "I can't go back to school because I don't have time" say "I have to go back to school because it's the only way to reach my goal." Once you believe that you have to do something your brain will send you constant reminders of what you have to do, and your negative thinking will be replaced with positive thinking.

Also, you have to have a reason for why you want to change your life, and you have to use that reason to motivate you to get things done. "I want to be successful because I don't want my family to struggle". Then every time you think about giving up remember the reason why you're doing it in the first place.

Also, I want you to start believing in yourself again. The kid inside of you still wants to be something and it's your job to make that kids dream come true. That greatness is still in you, but you're drowning it in misery and bitterness. Rescue it by going after your goals and dreams. Close your eyes and picture yourself as a kid. Picture yourself telling someone what you wanted to be when you grew up. Remember how you felt that day? You felt like anything was possible, and that you could be that one day. In that moment you didn't say what if, you didn't make excuses, you didn't think you weren't good enough, and you didn't say you couldn't do it. You just believed you could do it, and you believed that nothing would stop you from being it. Starting today, I need you to go back to being the kid who believed in themselves. The kid who made plans, not excuses. The kid who believed they could be anything in life because they were great, and they were good enough to be it.

Every day do something that will make you get closer to your goals. The closer you get the happier the kid inside you will be. Don't let life take away something you've dreamed of becoming your whole life. Don't let what happened to you ruin that kids dream. The kid in you is counting on you to make their dreams come true before their time is up. So, get busy, and don't let them down.

1. You can do it, you can do it, you can do it, you just have to believe in yourself.

2. What can you do now that will change your life or make it better?

3. Make that call, sign up, chase it, go after it, do it or get up; just don't give up.

4. Don't make excuses because excuses hold you back.

5. "A person that believes that there's nothing that they can't do has unlimited opportunities."

6. "Replace the 'I can't do it' attitude with the 'There's nothing that I can't do' attitude."

7. "You have to do things you don't want to do, to get to where you want to be."

8. "There's nothing that you can't do until you tell yourself that you can't do it."

9. "If you can learn there are plenty of things you can do with your life you just have to learn how to do them."

"Once a person realizes that they're the only person holding themselves back they'll realize that they are capable of many things."

"Don't ever think about killing yourself. You were put on earth for a reason. There are so many things that you can do with your life. You might feel empty, and you think no-one cares about you, but that's not true. A lot of good things can be waiting for you in the future. You might find love, you might have kids, and you might accomplish one of your goals. There are a lot of things you can do with your life. Maybe you can help other people who are going through what you're going through? Find a positive way to use your life. Don't give up just take things a day at a time."

THE TWENTY-FIFTH STEP

is to know your worth. Your worth isn't determined by how rich you are, or how you look or how rich you are. Just because someone is richer than you, it doesn't mean that their life is more important than yours. Never put anyone above you or think that someone is better than you because of their status or looks etc. You're important and you have the right to be happy just as much as they do. You also deserve to be treated with respect. Never think that you deserve to be treated like crap because of how you look or anything else. You have to love yourself enough to know that you're just as important as anyone else. Your worth is what you want it to be. You set your own standards; you decide what you will put up with and what you won't put up with. You're the boss of your life and what you say goes. You decide who stays in your life and who goes. Never let anyone treat you like crap because you deserve better than that. If you don't think you deserve better than that you need to raise your self-esteem and start loving yourself. Also, realize that what you put up with is what you think you're worth. If you're letting someone use you, walk all over you, abuse you, and cheat on you over and over again you don't know your worth. Learn your worth or you'll always be in relationships with people that don't love you or respect you. Don't lower your worth just to keep someone in your life. Don't accept disrespect just to keep them in your life.

Hold yourself accountable for the things you do, the choices you make and the things you allow. They can't hurt you over and over again unless you let them. They can't use you unless you give them something to use. Blame them for hurting you and blame yourself for putting up with it. Don't play the victim, and put all the blame on them. You can leave them at any time. If you choose to stay the blame falls on you.

THE TWENTY-SIXTH STEP

is to forgive yourself. Forgive yourself for all of your mistakes. We've all made mistakes in the past and we're all going to make mistakes in the future, but we can't let those mistakes ruin our whole life. Leave your mistakes in the past where they belong because you're on your way to new and better things. You can't undo your past mistakes, but you can learn from them and try to stop them from happening again in your future. Think about the people you've forgiven over and over again. You loved them so you forgave them for the bad choices they made, and you gave them another chance. Well, if you love yourself you need to forgive yourself, and give yourself another chance. Remember to always treat yourself the same way that you treat others.

THE TWENTY-SEVENTH STEP

is to focus on positive things and surround yourself with positive people. Positive people will motivate you to become a better you, and they'll help you to stay focused on your goals and other things you want to do in life. They will also have a positive attitude, and a positive outlook on life. When you hang around them their positivity will rub off on you, and motivate you to go after you own dreams and goals. If you hang around negative people they'll just keep you down, and just give you company when you're miserable. You need someone to pump you up and motivate you to get out of a hole; not someone that's going to join you in the hole and complain.

THE TWENTY-EIGHTH STEP

is to learn how to let go of everything that makes you miserable. Letting go doesn't mean that you're giving up or that you're not good enough it means that it's not meant to be or it's wrong for you. Let go of miserable people and miserable things so you can be happy. If someone is using you let them go. If they're walking all over you and holding you back let them go. Cutting negative people out of your life cuts down on the stress in your life. Once you learn how to cut negative people out of your life you'll be a lot happier and stress-free. Negative people like to keep you down with them so don't hold onto them or you'll be stuck where they're at.

"Moving on doesn't mean that it doesn't bother you anymore. It means you've decided that you're not going to let it ruin your whole life."

The TWENTY-NINTH STEP

is to realize that happiness is a state of mind. Happiness isn't about the material things you have it's about how you feel about yourself and your life. To be happy you have to find out what's making you unhappy and do something about it. Write down 5 things that you're unhappy about and do something about it. The more things you scratch off of your list the happier you'll be.

Until you're happy with your life and yourself you won't be happy. As I mentioned earlier you have to ask yourself "WHY AM I UNHAPPY?" then do something about those things so you can be happy. If you don't fix those things or accept them as is, you won't be happy. Never base your happiness on material things because you'll always think you need more things in order to be happy. Don't base your happiness on anything just live your life and enjoy all of the happy moments. Don't expect to be happy every day of your life because that is an unrealistic expectation.

Happiness

Every time you smile you're happy for just a moment, and in that moment you are taken away from pain. Well, happiness is enjoying the moments that make you smile. Every moment of your life won't be perfect. There are some moments that will make you hate life and other moments that will make you love life. You just have to enjoy the things you love and get through the things you hate. In life, you have to take the good with the bad. Happy people have bad days, but they know that day will pass and good days will come again. Happy people aren't happy 24/7, they have problems that get them down, and they have things they dislike about themselves or their life. However, they realize that their problems or dislikes aren't worth giving up on everything for. The things they love about life make life worth living for them. The thing is some people haven't found things that make life worth living for. They've given up on life, and they've decided that their life will always be a miserable one. Unlike happy people, miserable people think their problems make life not worth living. They let their problems stop them from loving life. They give up on everything because of their problems or flaws. Miserable people need to realize that they can't just sit back and wait for their life to change, they have to change it themselves. They can't have perfect days every day or a life without problems. To be alive is to have problems. To be alive is to have a bad day. A problem free person is a person that isn't living life to the fullest. For if they were living life to the fullest a problem would sure find them. To say you can't be happy because you have problems or flaws is to say that you'll never be happy because you'll always have those things. If you say that you're telling yourself that you're going to hate yourself and life for the rest of your life. That's a sad way to live life. Saying that life has to be perfect in order for you to be happy with it is an unrealistic demand. A demand that life will not give into no matter how much you hate it. You have to work with what life gives you, and chase after the things life doesn't give you. Miserable people expect life to be 100% perfect, and if it isn't perfect they hate it. Happy people know that life isn't 100% perfect, but they still make the best of it. Start making the best of what life has given you. Start appreciating what you already have, and start chasing the things you want to accomplish in life. Just because everything isn't going your way, and everything isn't perfect it doesn't mean that you should sit around and pout about it. Throw yourself a pity party because your life isn't great all the time. What have you done to make your life great? What have you done that could make your life the best life that it can be? Have you given life your all? Have you used your talents and the things you're good at to better yourself or your life? Have you chased after your goals and dreams? If you aren't doing anything that will make you proud of yourself or that will make you enjoy your life that's the reason you're so miserable. Realize that the happiest people are the people that chase after what makes them happy, and they focus on the things that make them happy. The most miserable people are the people that focus on negative things and hold onto the negative things in life.

When was the last time you did something positive with yourself or your life? Explain

Do you constantly focus on negative things or positive things? Explain

 If negative, then that's why you're so miserable. Negative people always look for the negative things about life, and they don't believe that there's anything positive about life. However, there are plenty of positive things about life, but they don't see them because they're too busy focusing on the negative things. Happiness is enjoying the happy moments, and not letting the bad moments stop you from living life to the fullest.

"Chase happiness, and run from misery"

THE THIRTIETH STEP

is to respect yourself and surround yourself with people that show you respect. Get rid of all of the disrespectful people in your love. You might love them, but if they keep disrespecting you they don't love you. Don't accept disrespect from anyone. Hold your head up high, put your foot down, and tell them that you don't put up with disrespect. It's your life and if someone doesn't treat you with respect they shouldn't be in it. If you accept their disrespect they'll never respect you. Strong people get respect and people that never stand up for themselves get walked over. Don't be afraid to say 'no' to people that try to take advantage of your kindness. Don't be nice to people that are walking all over you. Don't try to please people that don't appreciate you. If someone is treating you like crap cut them out of your life. If you put up with their disrespect you're telling them that it's okay to treat you like crap. You're also telling them that you don't love yourself. Demand respect or people will walk all over you. When you were a kid you knew your Dad would say 'No!' and your mom would say 'Yes!' So, you would ask your mom for everything because you knew you'd get your way. You would also try to get over on your Mom because you knew you'd get away with it. However, you knew not to try your dad or ask him for things because you knew he'd say no or punish you. So, if someone is walking all over you, it's because they know you'll put up with it, and let them get away with it. If you want respect you have to be like the dad I mentioned above. You have to be firm, and let people know that you won't put up with their crap. No-one can use you unless you're giving them something to use. If you stop giving it to them they can't use you.

"If they keep disrespecting you don't expect them to be loyal because loyalty requires respect"

THE THIRTY FIRST STEP

is to deal with your past. If you're running from something you need to deal with it. You can pretend like it isn't bothering you, but if you keep crying over it, it is bothering you. If you need to talk to a therapist, do it. Do whatever it takes to get it off your chest. If it's something really bad you might not ever get over it, but you can still get through it. Join a support group, talk to someone you trust or just write your thoughts down in a journal. Don't be afraid to tell your story. If you were a victim you shouldn't be ashamed of what happened to you. It wasn't your fault and it shouldn't have happened to you. Talking to other people is better than holding it in. If you hold it in it will eat you up inside, and destroy your self-esteem, self-worth, and life. I'm not telling you to get over it because some things you'll never get over, but I am saying that you can't let it ruin your whole life. In order to move on you have to use every ounce of your strength, and keep fighting through your tears. You can let what happened to you ruin your whole life or you can try your best to move on so you can be happy. They ruined your past, but they can't ruin your future unless you let them. Keep your head up, and defeat your enemies. If you defeated your past enemies, you can defeat your present and future enemies too. If you've been through a lot and you're still standing you're a strong person, and you have defeated your past enemies.

"Sometimes you have to be the hero that rescues themselves"

."

THE THIRTY-SECOND STEP

Are you holding a grudge against someone? _____

Should you let it go or hold onto it? _____

Is to let go of grudges. Most grudges are just simple misunderstandings that people have blown way out of proportion. Most grudges are over silly things, and if people would just sit down and talk about it, they could work things out. Never end a friendship or cut off a relative over something small. If someone owes you a small sum of money are you going to cut them off forever? Come on! Is that small amount of money worth their whole friendship? Don't cut people off for stupid reasons. Let go of the silly grudges you have, and be the bigger person about it.

If you cut them off for a good reason you still need to let go of your grudge towards them. Chances are they're not even thinking about you, and they have already moved on. So, there's no point in holding onto that grudge anymore.

"Never forget what's important in life! Material things can be replaced, but important people can't'

If you're holding a grudge against someone, are you going to let it go? Why are why not?

THE THIRTY-THIRD STEP

is to apologize to everyone you've wronged. If you did them wrong you need to own up to it, apologize for it, learn from it, and never do it again. If they choose not to forgive you at least you'll have closure, and you'll be able to close that chapter in your life. If you can't talk to them or apologize to them in person; just write your apology to them in a journal, and forgive yourself for what you did to them. Writing it down gets it off your chest, and forgiving yourself for it helps you to move on.

"You can't take back what you've said or done, but if you want closure you need to own up to it, apologize for it, and try to make it right.

Do you owe someone an apology? _____

Will you apologize to them? Why or why not?

THE THIRTY-FOURTH STEP

is to take care of yourself. A person who doesn't love themselves might not take care of themselves the way that they should. Since they dislike themselves they don't see the point in taking care of themselves. Realize that just because you dislike a few things about yourself that it doesn't mean that you should let the rest of yourself go. Taking care of yourself will make you feel better about yourself, and it's something you're supposed to do. Brush your hair, take a bath, and take care of your hygiene. Not loving yourself isn't an excuse to not take care of yourself the best that you can. Take care of yourself emotionally, mentally, and physically. Always be the healthiest you that you can be. If you have problems with your health listen to your doctor, and follow their instructions carefully. If you have an illness that can't be cured you can still take care of the other things in your life. Never let an illness take over your life and ruin it. You don't have to have perfect health to be happy. Just take care of yourself and keep fighting. Take things a day at a time. If you're addicted to illegal substances or you have other bad habits take steps to break that addiction. Take care of yourself so you can live as long as possible. If someone you loved were sick what would you do to take care of them? You would do everything you could for them. So, be willing to do everything for your own health as well.

What are three things that you can do that will better yourself?

1.

2.

3.

       Do those 3 things today. No Excuses

THE THIRTY-FIFTH STEP

is to not have unrealistic expectations. You have to accept that you'll have bad days every now and then. You have to accept that problems will pop up every now and then. Also, you have to accept that you'll make bad choices sometimes or even a few mistakes. Don't expect your life to be problem free and worry free 24/7. Just do your best to prepare for the bad days. When the bad days come don't stress too much just keep your head up and fight through them. Do you remember all of those other problems you fixed before? You know the problems you worried yourself over until you finally fixed them? Well, if you fixed those problems I'm sure you can fix your current and future problems too. Stay positive and deal with the bad days as they come. Strong people have bad days, but they keep fighting until they have good days again. Expect that things will happen, but also realize that you will fix them. It might take time and a lot of effort or strength but you'll get through it. Realize that you'll fall sometimes, but realize that you can get always get back up. Realize that you'll fail sometimes, but realize that you can always try again. Bad things are just speed bumps on your road to success, they might slow you down but you should never let them stop you. The only thing that should be able to stop you is death, but until then keep loving yourself and loving your life as best you can.

Learning how to love yourself starts with how your parents treat you, and it ends with how you treat yourself, how you let others treat you, and how you feel about yourself

As soon as you're done with this book go look in the mirror, and tell yourself that you love yourself. Then do one thing that proves that you will start taking care of yourself, protecting yourself and loving yourself. Below are a few suggestions.

1. If your house is messy clean your house until it's spotless.

2. If you've neglected your hygiene. Make yourself a nice bath and scrub yourself until you're super clean.

3. If you're holding onto someone that is using you or taking advantage of you. Protect yourself by deleting their number from your phone, and cutting them from your life. You can do it, and you deserve better.

4. If you've stopped caring about yourself. Spend more time preparing/grooming yourself for work, school or other activities.

5. If you never do anything for yourself. Shop online and treat yourself to something you like.

6. Write down a list of things you will do the next day to spoil yourself, take care of yourself or better yourself.

7. Fill out a job application online or call a school and asks about the career you're interested in.

8. Make a list of things you can do to reach your goal or goals, and start doing some of those things as soon as you get up tomorrow.

9. If you have an addiction look online for information on how to get rid of it.

10. Show yourself some love. Hang up a sign above your bed that says 'I LOVE ME UNCONDITIONALLY'

11. If you have a health problem. Make sure you're doing everything the doctor told you to do. Go drink 2 cups of water now and tomorrow make sure you drink 8.

12. You know that one thing that you keep putting off? The thing you keep saying you'll do tomorrow? Stop procrastinating, and get it done. Realize that procrastination holds you back, and it stops you from living the life you want to live. Start saying "I'll do it today" instead of "I'll do it tomorrow" and you'll finally get things done. Realize that you could be done with it by now or at least half-way done. Stop wasting time. Get it done. You're only hurting yourself.

Good Luck!

The paperback version of this book can be used in workshops, can be written in, has fill in the blank questions and answers, and is larger than most paperbacks.

If you like this book, please leave feedback

If you liked this book you'll love '25 STEPS TO LETTING GO OF SOMEONE YOU LOVE.'

"I love me and I know my worth" realize your self-worth

and '29 STEPS TO GETTING BACK ON YOUR FEET'

read my other books

'Dating Guide for Single Women'

Letting go of Mr. Wrong

'How Men can Avoid Getting Played'

'Dating Guide for Single Men'

'22 Steps to Moving on After Someone Hurts You'

'12 Steps to Learning How to Handle Rejection'

34 Steps to Losing Weight and Keeping it Off'

Table of Contents

PRELUDE

Table of contents

Unhappy humans

LOVE YOURSELF UNCONDITIONALLY

 Self-Love is unconditional love.

CONFIDENCE

 Confidence rule ONE

 Confidence Rule TWO

 Confidence rule THREE

 Confidence rule FOUR

 Confidence rule FIVE

 Confidence rule SIX

 Confidence rule SEVEN

 Confidence rule EIGHT

 Confidence Rule NINE

 Confidence Rule TEN

 Confidence Rule ELEVEN

 GET TO KNOW YOURSELF

 THE GOOD STUFF

 You've been there since day one

 Your worth isn't determined by your looks

 Don't punish yourself

 YOU'RE THE BOSS OF YOUR LIFE

 DON'T PILE YOUR PROBLEMS INTO ONE PILE

Determining your self-worth

Society

Controlled by Society

I Hate Myself

LIFE SUCK SOMETIMES

Today is a new day for you. It's the beginning of a new chapter in your life

5 REASONS PEOPLE DON'T LOVE THEMSELVES

LOVE AS YOU KNOW IT

THE FIRST STEP IN LOVING YOURSELF

THE SECOND STEP

THE THIRD STEP

THE FOURTH STEP

THE FIFTH STEP

Treat yourself right

Raining on your own parade

THE SIXTH STEP

THE SEVENTH STEP

THE EIGHTH STEP

A haters job is to HATE you

THE NINTH STEP

Who you really are

THE TENTH STEP

THE ELEVENTH STEP

THE TWELFTH STEP

THE THIRTEENTH STEP

THE FOURTEENTH STEP

THE FIFTEENTH STEP

THE SIXTEENTH STEP

THE SEVENTEENTH STEP

THE EIGHTEENTH STEP

THE NINETEENTH STEP

THE TWENTIETH STEP

The TWENTY-FIRST STEP

THE TWENTY-SECOND STEP

THE TWENTY-THIRD STEP

THE TWENTY-FOURTH STEP

THE TWENTY-FIFTH STEP

THE TWENTY-SIXTH STEP

THE TWENTY-SEVENTH STEP

THE TWENTY-EIGHTH STEP

The TWENTY-NINTH STEP

Happiness

THE THIRTIETH STEP

THE THIRTY FIRST STEP

THE THIRTY-SECOND STEP

THE THIRTY-THIRD STEP

THE THIRTY-FOURTH STEP

THE THIRTY FIFTH STEP

Printed in Great Britain
by Amazon